IN THE HAND
OF THE HOLY SPIRIT

In the Hand
of the Holy Spirit

The Art of J. B. Murray

Mary G. Padgelek

MERCER UNIVERSITY PRESS
Macon, Georgia

ISBN 0-86554-699-1   MUP/H518

The paper used in this publication meets the minimum requirements of American National Standard for Information Sciences—Permanence of Paper for Printed Library Materials, ANSI Z39.48-1984.

Library of Congress Cataloging-in-Publication Data

Padgelek, Mary Shaw Graham, 1952
    In the Hand of the Holy Spirit: The Art of J. B. Murray/ Mary G. Padgelek
        p. cm.
    Includes bibliographical references.
    ISBN 0-86554-699-1
    1. Murry, J. B. (John B.), 1908-1988—Criticism and interpretation. 2. Spirituality in art. 3. Afro-American artists—Georgia—Biography—History and criticism. 4. Outsider art—Georgia. I. Murry, J. B. (John B.), 1908-1988. II. Title

N6537.M874 P33 2000
760'.092—dc21
[B]
                                                            00-033929

CONTENTS

LIST OF ILLUSTRATIONS

Black and white photographs appear after page 20.

LIST OF COLOR PLATES

FOREWORDS

J. B. Murray was a friend of mine. Over the course of his life he was also a laborer, a sharecropper, a father, a mental patient, a religious mystic and an artist. It has been more than a decade now since his death, yet his legacy lives on in his art. So often he is referenced as "J. B. Murray, the outsider artist." In the pages that follow, Mary Padgelek has wonderfully documented this aspect of this amazing man. Let me tell you in a few words how I knew him.

I first met J. B. on 17 February 1977. He came to see me as a patient, complaining of some minor back pain or the like after failing to get relief from his previous physician. J. B. was of small stature, with fine smooth mahogany skin, and close cropped white hair. He sat in the straight backed chair in the exam room rather stiffly, dressed in a clean but faded green twill work shirt buttoned tightly at the collar, a worn suit coat that he reserved for such formal occasions as a visit to the doctor, durable khaki pants, and brogans. He was at once country-come-to-town but with a look in his eyes of infinite depth. I treated him that day and several other times over the ensuing months. Somehow—without specific words or negotiations—we became friends.

J. B. lived near the shoals of the Ogeechee in that most rural part of Georgia, which was probably more densely populated in the late eighteenth century than it is today. The land there can be coaxed to production, but the rolling hills of red clay and the sandy loam interspersed among them made for a hard life when the only source of income was agriculture. A few miles to the South one can see the deep ruts of the old National Highway authorized by Congress in the earliest days of the republic. Nearby are the few remaining ruins of Georgetown, the uppermost navigational point on the Ogeechee. Dispersed across the landscape are abandoned tenant houses, grown up hedgerows, and abandoned fields now planted in row upon row of loblolly pine. This environment was J. B.'s world.

I don't really specifically recall what prompted our friendship. Retrospectively, J. B. told others that he saw in me someone to help him take his message to the world. I recall that he once said (in so many words) that I had been one of the few in his lifetime who had treated him with more respect than his station in life might otherwise warrant. We were odd friends at that—the thirty-someish over-educated great grandson of slave owners and the illiterate farm laborer now living a subsistence life on a meager Social Security pension.

Sometimes J. B. was my wise man. I would complain and he would listen. Sometimes I helped him out. Life must have been better for J. B. at one time. I realized this when he was on the verge of having his land sold for unpaid taxes. Being totally illiterate, he had ignored the tax notices, insisting that he had sold all of his land except that tiny plot occupied by his self-built house. At one time he owned as much as 125 acres. Over the years this had been sold off a parcel at a time until almost nothing was left. The last buyer had failed to record the deed, allowing J. B. for years to pay taxes on land he no longer owned. He would borrow money with little hope of paying it back. I have in my files a terse note addressed simply to "J. B." from a local bank threatening foreclosure on nearly twenty-five acres of land for less than a thousand dollars in debt. We handled the problem.

As J. B.'s reputation as an artist grew, he changed little. His house—more of a shack— constructed of cast off and occasionally purchased building materials, grew and metamorphosed like an amoeba. The core section remained the same, but he seemed to be constantly building and changing. He would construct a room on one side only to tear it down months later in favor of another room on the other side of the house extending in the opposite direction. He continued to draw water by hand from his well. In a tiny garden protected from foraging rabbits on all sides by folded-up sheets of discarded roofing tin, he grew greens and collards. He bought an electric cook stove only to decide later that he preferred the wood-burning model.

J. B. had never been to Atlanta, even though he lived only two hours away by car. Actually, he first told me that he had been there, not wanting me to think him a bumpkin. It was only when I saw him marveling at the height of the buildings on Peachtree Street that he admitted that he had never seen such marvelous structures in all of his seventy-odd years. We had gone to see his work displayed in the Piedmont Park Art Festival. For the occasion he purchased a purple sharkskin suit, a purple shirt of only slightly different hue, and a fuzzy green fedora. We stood in silence in the gallery listening to the comments as viewers studied his work. After a short while he wanted to leave, saying something to the effect that, "They don't understand, do they?" We went back to the Peachtree Plaza Hotel, rode the elevator to the revolving restaurant at the top, and had a glass of iced tea.

J. B. relished the attention that his drawings brought to him, but he remained true to his mission. To him, and to each of those who had come to truly know the salvation that is available only through the Lord, his works were hymns of praise. He produced graphic abstract representations of the eternal dichotomies of good and evil, God and man, heaven and hell, each with a clear message for those who knew God and indecipherable to those who refused His eternal salvation.

Near the end of his life as his cancer became progressively more painful and it was evident that he was dying, he worked feverishly to somehow finish telling the world his message of salvation through the Lord. He talked with me about dying. He talked about judgment day, when the dead shall arise and all souls, black and white, shall stand before the Lord. He worried about heaven, thinking that perhaps he had not done enough in this life to be acceptable before God. Toward the end, on a hot August afternoon I visited J. B. at his daughter's house where he had moved after he became too weak to care for himself. I was ushered in to see him as he lay on a narrow cot in a dark paneled room lighted only by a shaft of sunlight through an open window. He had been working on a "book," writing in his indecipherable script a final opus on life and death. He wanted me to read it, as always believing that I could understand what he wanted to tell the world. He picked up the manuscript and held it out to me to begin to explain what he had written. He then paused, silent for a moment, lowered the book and said, "But you understand, don't you?" I lied to him, telling him that I did. I have been trying to do so ever since.

William Rawlings, M.D.
Sandersville, Georgia

Trying to understand J. B. Murray is like trying to comprehend an elephant from various descriptions of the seven blind men. During his creative years he was visited by a handful of interested individuals—writers, artists, art dealers, and collectors. Those of us who knew J. B. were deeply moved by who we thought he was and by the work he did. However, we all saw Mr. Murray through the veil of our own preconceptions. Although Murray was a simple, quiet, unassuming, and deeply religious man, he has had a major influence on the evolution of ideas in twentieth century art. This has come about not because of J. B.'s definition as a visionary, or a self-taught folk artist, or outsider, but simply because of the quantity, quality, and singularity of the artwork he produced during a short ten-year period of time.

In this book, Mary Padgelek has done a remarkable job of fitting together the pieces of the puzzle from the facts of Murray's life, his relationships to the local community, to the art world, and to our society as a whole. As it should, her focus remains on the work itself and she gives an in-depth evaluation of the formal aspects of Murray's art. That Dr. Padgelek is the right person to do this is evidenced by her ability to maintain a clear connection between the physical and spiritual presence in Murray's work and by her obvious belief in the power and meaning of this art. Murray believed that he was chosen to convey the message of God. He believed that God moved his hand when he wrote or painted. Murray clearly indicated that he thought we were sent to help him deliver this message. Although Mary Padgelek never actually met J. B., it is certain that he would have considered her to be called forth in order to help him spread his word, his message, or as he was convinced, God's message.

My first introduction to Murray's work occurred in the fall of 1982. Every semester I show my art class at the University of Georgia a survey of the work of visionary artists ranging from American folk art to fantastic environments, to examples of European "art brut" and so called psychopathological art from the Prinzhorn Collection in Germany. One of my students, Krista Rawlings, came to me after class and said that she thought I might be interested in some material that a patient of her husband's had been bringing to him for some time. The next week she came with a box full of Murray's writings. These were done on various non-archival materials ranging from scraps of cardboard to cash register tape to pages torn out of a pocket Bible. There were hundreds of pages of indecipherable writing that occasionally broke up into pattern and figure-like forms with dots for eyes. From the beginning, Murray's art was remarkable in its intensity and uniqueness of vision. It did, however, share some general elements with the work of artists that I had shown my class, especially Murray's scriptolaliac writings, which could compare to the cabalistic lettering of the great visionary James Hampton or with some obsessive mediumistic markings of European artists in the Prinzhorn Collection.

That weekend I drove to Sandersville, Georgia, where I met Krista's husband, Dr. William Rawlings, Jr., and he took me to meet J. B. for the first time. I came away from the meeting with a clear sense that Murray was genuinely involved in an intense, ongoing, religious phenomenon that had been set in motion by a major visionary experience. He was the real thing. He had received an epiphany and it had changed his life forever.

It is not entirely clear what Murray thought about the writing and drawing that he was obsessively producing. I am quite sure that he did not regard this work as art. He was clear, however, that he did not take personal responsibility for what his hand produced and that he believed that he was an instrument of God. When questioned about the drawings, he would offer some explanation that had a quasi-Christian narrative. It seemed to me that his explanation was given more to satisfy the person asking the question rather than from a personal conviction. I think that Murray tried to apply a Christian framework onto his work, perhaps to understand it better himself, but more because he wanted us to believe his motivations were good. His drawings were reflections of his inner vision, and the hours and hours he spent working on them were a meditative way of connecting to an inner state that brought him closer to his original and major vision.

As more and more people came to see him, he was always pressed to offer more explanations of what his drawings meant. For most, it was not enough to see that these works were profound and beautiful manifestations of a profound and beautiful personal experience. It was not enough to accept the possibility that Murray really was channeling a higher power. It was not enough to realize that Murray's intuitive use of formal elements, line, color, composition, repetition, and form, was exceptionally brilliant. It was not enough to believe that Murray's calm, quiet persona was the result of a sage-like inner peace, connected to an insight into the infinite. Murray was constantly asked to interpret what must have been an imponderable experience that words could never approximate. Consequently J. B. may have tried to give his visitors what he thought they wanted rather than what he truly felt. This could have also been true when he talked with me.

Murray was always sincere. He did not lie. He did not preach. He believed deeply in the power of his work. He had an enlightened relationship to the immediate environment that he had lived in all his life. He brought water out of the ground to nourish his spiritual as well as his physical health. Keeping a small bottle of his water near him was a way of containing a symbol of faith. To some he explained that the water enabled him to read his writing or to divine truth. To me he said simply that the water was "what Jesus walked on," a moving manifestation of the power of belief and faith. I think this is a deep and subtle understanding of a cosmic principle. All matter is constantly changing, but water, with its transparent but reflective qualities and its perpetual flowing, seems to reveal the numinous in such a perfect way.

It makes sense that through his heritage Murray's use of water, and various other elements of his art, might be connected to practices of tribal peoples from the West Coast of Africa. In matters of the spirit, African-Americans have influenced many aspects of American life. That we might not be able to trace a direct provable link to African practices could suggest that this influence can surface in certain individuals from a source that would be collective in nature. Murray's belief in his hand being directed by a higher force would certainly support this notion. It is not difficult to find relationships between Murray's art and the art of other visionary cultures. Most all transcendental religious art shares an obsession with surface pattern, horror vaccui, and the use of writing or calligraphy as a visual element. Religious art reflects the religious experience. The commonalties of this art across various cultures reveals its archetypal nature. The obsessive patterning of Murray's and almost all mediumistic art simply reflects what science is discovering in nature, that behind the apparent chaos of the universe lie hidden patterns and infinite layers of meaning. I believe J. B. Murray was given a glimpse of this wondrous world and that his art is an incredible manifestation of his sage-like vision. Now at the end of the twentieth century we need more than ever to find, understand, and believe the message of special individuals like Murray. Mary Padgelek has given us much more than an artist's biography. She has, through the life and work of Murray, given us another reason why faith, hope, and deep belief are so important to this world. Through the reproductions she has also given us the opportunity to see for ourselves how eloquently Mr. Murray's work speaks for itself.

Andy Nasisse
University of Georgia

In his eulogy for J. B. Murray's funeral in September 1988, Reverend J. A. Bryant, pastor of Hickory Grove Baptist Church, said that this master visionary had "left no unfinished business." His

that this master visionary had "left no unfinished business." His surviving descendants—three daughters, four sons, two sisters, twenty-nine grandchildren and great grandchildren—paid tribute to him with a reading titled *Waited*: "Daddy, there is a shadow that awaited you somewhere around the bend, there sweet whispers and gentle peace shall welcome you in. . . ."

Two and a half years earlier, in April 1986, having received directions to his house from Andy Nasisse, I drove to see Murray in Mitchell, Georgia. The man I met that day was someone whose life had been profoundly changed by a visionary experience eight years earlier. After that experience, his faith had become embodied rather than intellectualized, and he had begun recording what he called "the language of the Holy Spirit direct from God." Because of his age he could no longer do the physical labor of planting and working his farm, but he seeded pages of stationery with a glossolalic script and repeatedly stroked bright columns of paint on cardboard, cast off objects, and drawing paper. Visiting him and later interviewing him on video tape, it seemed that his voice, his face, and the paintings he made became a luminous spectrum in which image and effect were seamlessly reconciled.

Our conversations consisted of spontaneous prayers that Murray improvised on the spot, sometimes singing, sometimes speaking, with short breaks in response to my questions: "When did you start to paint? Did God come to you at once or slowly?" This is an example of one of his answers:

When I started I prayed and I prayed and the Lord sent a vision from the sun. Everything I see is from the sun. He showed me signs and seasons, and he tells me. Then he turned around and gave me a question to ask him. And when I asked him, I wanted to see my mother. He brought her before me and two brothers. And then again he gave me a mind to ask him again, and I asked him again. And the three come up as a shadow, a spiritual shadow, ain't like us, ain't like our bodies.

The soothing shadow of the Spirit and the driving light of the Spirit—J. B. Murray knew them both. The script, the paintings, the songs and words were not so much descriptions of his charismatic experience as extensions of it. His attitude was rooted in a specific event, but the call to action had come slowly, "in a vision, a likeness," he said. Eventually he began to write "the language of the Holy Spirit" and make paintings. What emerged was the embodiment of devotion rather than the representation of a memory. The results were beautiful and physically remarkable.

The plowing of the ground, the columnar marking of paper—many elements of Murray's art, as well as his speech, were mantra-like and repetitive like the revolving of the earth sustaining its progression across the sun with alternating cycles of shadow and light marking the passage of time. "God put the instrument in my hands and rules and guides my hands to do this," Murray said. "He moves my fingers, I can't move them on my own. Jesus, make an instrument of my fingers! Lord, go over our minds!" The strength of his devotion and the clarity of his purpose must surely have had a physical effect on the organization of time in the rhythms of line and form that materialized in front of him. Surely the faith he brought to the act of painting had a profound effect on its consequences.

One visible characteristic of "the language of the Holy Spirit"—its "abstraction"—made Murray virtually unique among artists of his time and circumstance. But in discussions of his faith, he would return to archetypes of enlightenment almost universally expressed in celestial imagery: "Everything I see is from the sun." In some instances, fellow Christians recognized their core belief in the sound of this phrase. Such parallels were commonplace in the speech of a man who rendered dichotomies like sacred/secular or art/artifact pointless.

The collectors who visited Murray influenced the volume of works he was able to make but had little if any effect on their content. However, Murray was aware of the contextual shift that occurred when his paintings left him and he was enthusiastic about carrying God's word to the world at large: "That's all I can tell. I'm not to take from and I'm not to add, just do what the Spirit said do. . . . It was the Lord that used me and changed these writings and different letters and drawings. That's like he gives us different verses and prayers and psalms—the same." This was as close as we ever came to discussing "the language of the Holy Spirit" as art.

Today, many years after J. B. Murray's death, I have come to believe that his devotional attitude, his clarity of purpose, and the convergence of African and American traditions in his art are among the characteristics that distinguish him from individuals who are simply eccentric or delusional and that these qualities reinforce the far-reaching influence he is having on contemporary American art. Towards the end of his life, "the language of the Holy Spirit" traveled to where Murray, in bodily form, could not go. First, into the hands of his neighbors, then to the minds of those of us who felt compelled to seek him out, and later to exhibitions and art collections around the world. The energies released in this process have intensified with the passage of time. They cut through stringently constructed realities that might otherwise have limited them.

Mary Padgelek's study is the first to systematically examine the integrity of Murray's practice in the context of these developments. Her research is unique in its acknowledgment and examination of the different points of view that have come to bear on the meaning of his art. She does this without sacrificing the mystery at the heart of her subject. J. B. Murray was a bright light who cast a long shadow. Those of us who were privileged to have spent some time with him will never forget him. We were changed by him, he kept us growing, and he strengthened and affirmed the human condition.

Judith McWillie
University of Georgia
Athens, Georgia

ACKNOWLEDGMENTS

I am indebted to many people who have generously shared their time and ideas with me throughout the course of my research on J. B. Murray. Dr. Sandy Martin from the Department of Religion at the University of Georgia and an expert on southern religion has been invaluable for augmenting my historical understanding of evangelical Protestantism. He also suggested excellent resources for the history of the faith and the difference between an African-American understanding of evangelicalism and a European-American approach to the faith. These resources broadened my understanding of the faith that informed Murray's art. I am grateful to Dr. Evan Firestone for his input from an art history criticism perspective that challenged me to view Murray in the light of contemporary thinking. I am grateful to Dr. Janice Simon for her excellent ideas and her own high standards that consistently challenged me and added depth and rigor to my thinking. It was in her art history class at the University of Georgia that I first discovered J. B. Murray and became excited over Murray's art and the ever-opening story of his life-changing vision.

Dr. Robert Nix offered an understanding of the spirit of my research that continually uplifted, informed, and enlightened my thinking. Through his years of teaching Sunday school, his own study of the Bible, his deep understanding, and his personal practice of Christian principles, he offered me an in-depth discernment of the faith that comprises the essence of understanding J. B. Murray. Professor Judith McWillie's friendship with Murray, her personal understanding of him as an artist and as a person of deep conviction, her generosity in sharing her notes, her slides of Murray's work, and her videotaped interview with Murray have given this book on J. B. Murray a comprehensiveness that would have been impossible without her input. Her knowledge of the world of art and ideas about what Murray and other self-taught visionaries offer to the future of American art have given me valuable perspective. Her scholarly comprehension of the art of the self-taught visionaries and her spiritual understanding of these artists and their work, which she has shared with me through many interviews, have been an inestimable part of my work on J. B. Murray.

Professor Andy Nasisse has also made this book possible through his generosity in sharing his understanding of Murray, his slides of Murray, and his time in working with me during our numerous meetings and interviews. Nasisse also shared with me his profound comprehension of Murray and other self-taught visionaries, how they affect the world of art, and what they offer to people that accounts for their current popularity. Dr. William Rawlings was invaluable to this research in sharing his personal knowledge of Murray, letting me view and photograph the work he had of Murray's, and his generous accounts of his understanding of and relationship with Murray as his physician and friend. Rawlings introduced me to members of the community and Murray's family, who gave me information about Murray from a perspective outside of the world of art.

I wish to thank Murray's family and the residents of Mitchell, Georgia, who talked with me about Murray as they knew him both before and after he had a vision and began his art. I particularly want to thank Mrs. Sara Murray Pinkston, Murray's sister-in-law, and Mrs. Ellen Murray Lindsey, his daughter, who offered their time and their perspectives on Murray. These interviews portrayed him as a member of his community and family and helped to complete the portrait of J. B. Murray beyond his role as an artist, adding greatly to my comprehension of him as a person.

Finally, I would like to acknowledge the persons whose financial support allowed me to include the color illustrations of Murray's art. They are Mr. Robert Hart, Dr. William Rawlings, and Mr. Steve Slotin. I value all of the people whose support and generosity have made this book on J. B. Murray possible.

Murray was very complex. He was an internal, deeply obsessed individual. He had a light shining through him and his work. The aesthetic success he had had to do with his level of engagement. He couldn't fail. When you're that engaged in the dynamics of the visionary experience, it's just too honest, it's too real. You can't fail.
—Andy Nasisse

J. B. was very happy about all of this. He would come to me and tell me about his visions and what God had told him. It just had to be from God; how else would this thing happen? How else could he do it? Maybe the Holy Spirit really did move his hand.
—Sara Murray Pinkston

The Holy Spirit comes to do the Lord's work. I have faith. He is no other help I know. There is nothing He starts but what He don't finish.
—J. B. Murray

1

INTRODUCTION:
J. B. MURRAY AND THE POWER OF BELIEF

Now we see but a poor reflection as in a mirror; then we shall see face to face.
—1 Corinthians 13:12

In his early seventies, J. B. Murray (1908-1988), an African-American man from rural Georgia who could neither write nor read, suddenly began to write, paint, and draw flowing yet often erratic abstractions.[1] (See illustrations 1 and 2 and color plate 1.) Believing that he had received a vision from God, Murray began to create his art. The abstraction of Murray's compositions distinguishes them from work by other visionary self-taught artists whose figurative paintings express their spirituality. Murray created ghostly figures with transfixed eyes and long, vertical bodies that converge toward the center of a painting of brightly colored abstraction. To Murray these elongated shapes were "the people what is lying, them is the people what is living like God don't exist."[2] He often repeated the words, "Give me a louder word up," as he looked through a jar of well water at his colorful daubs of paint, erratic dots,

---

[1] The spelling *Murry* is often used instead of *Murray*. *Murry* is a spelling William Rawlings and Murray agreed upon, but I have chosen to use *Murray* because this is the way his parents and family spell the name and his daughter Ellen prefers the family spelling. Also the *Murry* spelling is somewhat linked to Murray's being defined as an outsider artist, a definition with which I disagree.

[2] Transcript (in author's possession) of J. B. Murray, interview with Judith McWillie, video recording, Mitchell GA, 31 May 1985.

and his script hidden in between larger shapes.[3] Murray repeated these words, at times almost like a chant. To him the work was "the language of the Holy Spirit direct from God."[4]

Murray's manifestation of his "call" does not involve depicting the recognizable components of his evangelical Christian faith, such as the parables of Jesus, other stories of biblical characters, or prophecies from the Book of Revelation. Instead, Murray's expression emanated from his unconscious, revealing a state between dream and reality. His imagery emerged not solely from his intellect operating on external reality, but arose out of dreams and visions. Murray's mind transformed reality and produced an inner image purified of superfluous detail. He had a personal revelation or some sudden, internal impetus that led to his creative production. For some artists, visions can be compared to inspiration, yet to Murray spiritual appearances provided such an intensity as to offer the primary motivation for the last ten years of his life and his art.

The visionary artist throughout history has sought, directly or indirectly, to offer a glimpse of the eternal amidst a temporal world. Art that is spiritually inspired has reminded people throughout time that there exist those who believe they respond to another dimension and seek to express this understanding through the visual arts. Such artists are assumed to possess a visionary style of gathering information from their lives; they believe they are able to see a divine connection to the human realm, the infinite in the midst of the finite, the spiritual enclosed in the material. Many people viewing the work of visionary artists respond to the art's formal aspects and do not care about the message the art seeks to communicate. Others, after viewing the initial attraction of an artist's work, desire to understand its meaning.

Without a key to a visionary artist's symbols, however, the art can be "but a poor reflection as in a mirror," and the spiritual world of the

---

[3]The words, "Give me a louder word up" that Murray used, indicate his beseeching the wisdom of the Holy Spirit to affect his counsel to the people who visited him.

[4]Murray, transcript of videotaped interview.

artist an unintelligible mystery. This book seeks to unveil the symbols, impetus, and meaning of the work of J. B. Murray, who created his work through the inspiration of his perceptions of eternity. Murray believed his art offered a redemptive metaphor for spiritual healing, regeneration, and ultimate salvation. The message within Murray's art, although seemingly unreadable, is ensconced in the teachings of a faith that has as a primary mission to reach out to people with the hope of salvation and deliverance. His bold, colorful abstractions entice the viewer aesthetically, while the message of the art strikes at the core of a world-view that has historic American religious roots.

In a vision, Murray saw the sun come down to him and a spiritual eagle crossed his eye. He believed afterwards that the eagle's passage allowed him to discern things that other people could not comprehend. He saw Jesus on a cloud and knew that God had set him apart for a special work. His creativity came from an unknown place where the heart hears a word—who knows from where—and the body and soul ignite into a unified life-changing passion. His words and haunted images flowed from a faith that God had a message—and Murray carried the message to anyone who came to him to witness and benefit from his evocation of the Holy Spirit.

His art hints at the existence of another dimension beyond common awareness. His belief that the Holy Spirit had chosen him for a specific evangelical mission was the stimulus that opened the door to his innate creativity. His faith did not produce the talent he displayed or his aesthetic sensibilities, but it did ignite his natural creativity and gave him a powerful reason to communicate fervently through the vehicle of art with all the potency of a spiritual awakening.

Within seven years after Murray began his first marks on discarded materials, his art was being shown nationally and internationally and was included in collections all over the world. Some of the public collections that include Murray's art range from the Embassy Art Collection in Washington DC, to the Outsider Archives, London, England, the High Museum of Art, Atlanta, Georgia, and the Museum of American Folk Art in New York City, to name a few.

How a farm worker in rural Georgia, within a ten year period of time, rose to be an artist whose work is included in national and international exhibits and collections is a cause for wonder. Murray shared the message of salvation through his figures, expressed his veneration for the Word of God through his script, and counseled people in his home through what he believed to be the guidance of the Holy Spirit. His paintings are the manifest heralds of redemptive praise, jeremiads postulating demise by way of his numerous haunting figures that stare out from polymorphous abstractions and script that gives the instructions of salvation, while the Holy Spirit is believed to inspire the words of advice Murray gives to his visitors. His evangelical view of the world not only gave him a reason to create, but deeply influenced the form, components, and ritual connected to his art.

We might ask what specifically makes Murray an artist worthy of our visual and aesthetic admiration. Are his belief system and his sincerity factors in the appreciation of his art? The answer to this question is both yes and no. Murray's beliefs and purpose behind his art are factors that cannot be separated from his work, despite the Western art historic tendency to isolate the art from its purpose, tradition, and core inspiration. These entities are a part of Murray's art that add richness and understanding to his images. Conversely, belief does not make art good or bad. Although Murray's belief produced his art, sincerity is not enough to make art worthy of aesthetic admiration. Murray's worthiness as an artist involves his formal success. As you will see in this book, his compositions are intuitively well designed as color and form are repeated throughout a painting with a dynamic energy. His images are arresting and draw the viewer into their mystery with beguiling faces. Murray used art materials in a sophisticated method of layering that has a remarkable visual complexity. The artistic vision he created has the consistency of a mature, fully-developed style. Murray created from the depth of his personality; such is the source of authentic art. An appreciation of the formal success of Murray's work and an understanding of what he desired to communicate are, therefore, both necessary to begin to comprehend his art and his power of belief.

2

A VISION FROM THE SUN:
PORTRAIT OF A VISIONARY

Our lives are fashioned, not by our intentions, but by responding to these invitations that come from fate, and from other people and events, mysteriously. And I think that what art can do that reason can't do is provide us with images that help us contemplate these mysteries.
—Thomas Moore [1]

Born on 5 March 1908, to John H. Murray and Moriah Macrae M. Bass in Warren County, Georgia, John Bunion Murray made a quiet entry into the small, rural town of Mitchell, Georgia. He attended a public school in Warren County at the age of six for one month and from the age of six until the late 1970s when he retired, he worked as a general farm laborer. In 1929 Murray married Cleo Kitchens and they had eleven children, five of whom died before Murray.[2] At the time of his death, the Murray family consisted of sixteen grandchildren, thirteen great grandchildren, and three great, great grandchildren. Murray's wife Cleo died in September 1987 after a ten-year illness.[3] At the beginning of her illness (approximately 1977) she had gone to live with one of the children and was likely not aware of Murray's artistic production.[4] Murray was diagnosed with prostate cancer in 1984, but did not show

---

[1]Thomas Moore, "The Liminal Zones of Soul," in Suzi Gablik, *Conversations Before the End of Time* (New York: Thames and Hudson, Inc., 1995), 409.

[2]Sara Murray Pinkston, interview with author, tape recording, Mitchell GA, 20 July 1993.

[3]Ellen Murray Lindsey, telephone conversation with author, 22 December 1995.

[4]Ibid.

symptoms of this illness until 1987.[5] He died at the Memorial Hospital in Washington County, Georgia, on 18 September 1988.

Murray lived with his son Ray after retirement, during which time he built a separate house on the same property around 1978. His small home (illustration 3), which was little more than a simple shed, had indoor plumbing added after his art brought in some income beyond his social security check. He grew his own food in his garden and drew water from a well in his yard (illustration 4). The land Murray and his son lived on was somewhat isolated, although subdivisions existed a few miles away. Murray's daughter Ellen, who took care of him at the end of his life, lived in a nearby neighborhood.

The town of Mitchell had only one store, a combination convenience and hardware store as well as a gas station. Located within close driving distance of his house, this business was the primary source of Murray's various art and general supplies throughout his life. Most people knew or had heard of one another in Mitchell, and the members of the community worked primarily as farmers, farm laborers, or as workers in the pulpwood industry. The various churches of the community comprised the centers of social activity as well as worship.

Murray was a member of Mineral Springs Baptist Church and lived in a part of the community called Four Corners, where Glascock, Hancock, Washington, and Warren counties meet. His house was in Glascock County near the fall line of the Ogeechee River where people commonly approach the water to go rafting or to enjoy the shoals. Glascock County was a predominantly white county in the midst of an area called the "Black Belt." The "Black Belt" derived its name from the fact that African-Americans dominated this four-county area politically, culturally, socially, and religiously. In Glascock County, a small, sparsely-populated area that consists of 170 square miles, the black families were generally known because of their small numbers, and the black population, characteristically, did not move in or away. Generation after generation of African-American

[5]William Rawlings, telephone conversation with author, 17 January 1996.

families were born and raised in the same locale. They made up a self-contained community separate from the larger population of whites. Murray farmed on a white person's land, but rarely mixed with whites socially or religiously.[6]

In spite of the fact that many poor whites and poor blacks who lived in the four-county area shared a relatively equal economic status, Glascock County had a history of poor race relationships. At the turn of the century, whites ran most of the black tenant farmers out of Glascock County when resentment arose between the races because blacks worked for lower wages, and whites were not being hired as farm workers and tenant farmers.[7] This conflict apparently accounts for the small number of African-American families in Glascock County as compared to the African-American majorities in the other three counties.

Murray grew up, raised a family, and later produced his art in an area where both white and black citizens knew him and knew his family through several generations. He left this area only once, when he and William Rawlings, his physician and friend from nearby Sandersville, went to Atlanta when Murray was included in a group art exhibition at the Piedmont Art Festival in 1986.

A Portrait of a Visionary

One might wonder if the seeds for the visionary experience were present for Murray prior to age seventy, yet little evidence points to anything unusual about him before this time. From the words of various people who knew him, the portrait of a gentle, sensitive man usually emerges, but not a man prone to ecstatic religious manifestations or known for his involvement with any artistic production.

---

[6]Carolyn Fordham, interview with author, tape recording, Mitchell GA, 20 July 1993.
[7]Phinizy Spalding, telephone conversation with author, 1 July 1993. Spalding, an expert on the colonial history of Georgia, contributed research on Georgia's colonial history in the book, A History of Georgia, Kenneth Coleman, ed. (Athens: The University of Georgia Press, 1982).

Murray did change, however. No one can offer an explanation of that fact, only confirmation.

Sara Murray Pinkston, Murray's neighbor and sister-in-law, described Murray both before and after his vision as "a good, kind man who was always helpful."[8] Sara worked on the same farm as Murray for many years and they knew each other well. She was married to Murray's brother Plee. She gave examples of Murray's going out of his way to do favors for people in need. For instance, Murray offered people rides in his truck whether convenient for him or not, and he frequently fixed broken equipment for friends. She said that Murray was always religious, but she described him as quiet and somewhat shy. Concerning Murray's behavior after his vision, Sara stated:

> He [Murray] said that his writing would spell words like G-O-D spaced out. He would get a message through the water. He never did this with me, but I knew he did it. I think he had a little ol' bottle he'd look through and say that God was telling him and showing him things through that water. God would tell him what to say and do. He didn't change except for doing this work.[9]

Additionally, Carolyn Fordham, a retired school teacher who grew up in Mitchell, Georgia, and knew Murray and his family for many years, stated that the Murrays were a very moral, honest family who were poor but well respected in the community.[10] She commented that before Murray retired, he worked twelve to fourteen hours a day to feed his family. University of Georgia art professor Judith McWillie, who met Murray around 1984 and visited him quite a few times at his home in Glascock County, stated that everybody she met in the area knew Murray and thought of him as a gentle person, but also as an

---

[8]Pinkston interview.
[9]Ibid.
[10]Fordham interview.

enigma—a mystery. From others' descriptions of him it was obvious to McWillie that he was not an outspoken member of his community.[11] Similarly, Leona Lundy, a woman who is the age of some of Murray's children and who had been a neighbor of Murray's at an earlier time, was aware of his later visionary experience and his art. She said that Murray did not stand out in regard to his religious fervor before 1978, although he regularly attended church and was considered a strong Christian. However, after 1978, Murray's religious zeal was openly apparent as he underwent a change that Leona witnessed but did not understand.[12] Andy Nasisse, an art professor from the University of Georgia who met Murray in 1982 and was instrumental in introducing him to the art community, further described Murray as a solitary person who lived simply but well. "He lived close to the land and ate vegetables from his garden watered by the same well from which he would later fill his jar of water he looked through to interpret his paintings."[13] Nasisse believed that Murray did not have much emotional support from his family and community before the advent of his art.[14]

Murray's family and friends have speculated about what happened to him in 1978 to transform a quiet, rather shy, retired farm worker into a man with a single-minded devotion to what he believed was a calling with uncertain destination. Colored abstract paintings and an indecipherable script stand as testimony to an occurrence that can be anchored to a certain year and a specific place. We can know the date and the locale, yet to understand the experience we must turn to the words of the artist himself.

The Vision

In his essay, "The Poet," Ralph Waldo Emerson wrote:

---

[11]Judith McWillie, telephone conversation with author, 28 June 1993.
[12]Leona Lundy, interview with author, tape recording, Mitchell GA, 20 July 1993.
[13]Andy Nasisse, interview with author, tape recording, Athens GA, 18 January 1995.
[14]Ibid.

I conceive that a person is always spoken to from behind and is unable to turn and see the speaker. If he listens with insatiate ears, richer and greater wisdom is taught him. His health and greatness consist in his being the channel through which heaven flows to earth, and an ecstatical state takes place in him.[15]

J. B. Murray listened with such "insatiate ears" that he believed the voice of God spoke to him in a vision. To him this vision truly initiated him as the "channel through which heaven flows to earth." He believed that he acted as a vessel for God's Spirit and that this Spirit moved his hand on the page to produce approximately 1,500 to 2,000 paintings and untold pages filled with a mysterious script.

Murray lived with his son Ray in a small wooden house at the time of his first vision. His son also had a woman friend who was living in the house with them. Murray had been retired less than a year at this time and kept busy with small projects. There were items such as buckets of house paint and brushes, old appliances, and scrap building materials in the yard. His wife Cleo had not lived with him for several years because of an illness and had gone to live with one of their daughters. He and Cleo were married for over sixty years at the time of his vision. Their eleven children were grown and most of them had families of their own.[16]

Murray would often visit his sister-in-law Sara Murray Pinkston. She and Murray remained close friends after her husband, Murray's brother, died. Since she and Murray used to work on the same farm for many years, their friendship spanned many decades. She was the first person Murray talked to about his "call" after he had his initiating vision.[17]

On a warm May afternoon in 1978, Murray was watering his potatoes with a garden hose, a task he performed every few after-

---

[15]Ralph Waldo Emerson, "The Poet," *The Collected Works of Ralph Waldo Emerson*, vol. 3 (Cambridge: Belknap Press, 1983).

[16]Pinkston interview.

[17]Ibid.

noons. He was alone, as he was most afternoons now. He described that as he watched the water spray the ground, he suddenly saw the sun come down to him, turning his hands and everything around him yellow. There were also rainbow colors all around him.[18] His words describe this first vision, which was the experience that initiated his art production, "Well, I was out in the yard working on the potato patch and the sun came right to me. Had different colors even around my hands turned kinda yellow, like different color ground. Well, I prayed and I took up a water hose, hosed up the sun and the rainbow come to me."[19] Murray described seeing Jesus coming down in the clouds as he looked up at the sky, and this was when he believed he saw the eagle that flew across his eyes that he connected with being able to "see things other folks can't see."[20] He also described hearing the voice of his dead mother asking Jesus to "take care of my child," referring to Murray.[21]

At some point soon after this vision, Murray used the paint, brushes, pens, scrap paper, and supplies around his house to create his first script and painted marks. Pinkston described Murray as he first came over to her house to tell her about his vision and "call" as being puzzled about what God wanted him to do, yet excited.[22] He showed her the script and "read" it to her. Every time he had a new vision he would visit her and tell her. She worried about him and was afraid he was losing his mind, at first. Then she saw how happy it made him and decided this experience was for the good.[23]

Through continuing visions and/or auditory messages he believed were from God, Murray understood that God was calling him to move his hand as the Holy Spirit led him. Initially, Murray had no idea in what direction these visions would lead him. However, through

---

[18]Transcript (in author's possession) of J. B. Murray, interview with Judith McWillie, video recording, Mitchell GA, 31 May 1986.
[19]Ibid.
[20]Ibid.
[21]Ibid.
[22]Pinkston, interview.
[23]Ibid.

continual visions he came to believe that the figures in his work were people who lived without God. Murray believed that God wanted him to warn people to turn back and seek salvation.[24] He talked about God giving him the writing and that he was "not to add to or take away, but do what the Spirit said to do."[25] He also equated the different kinds of writing and the different letters with "the different folks who don't respect God. God gives me these different letters for these folks."[26] He had difficulty believing God thought he was important enough to honor him with this work. "Jesus, I didn't know I was close enough to you for you to bless me with this work."[27]

Shortly after Murray had his initial vision, he presented his script in sealed envelopes and on adding machine tape to the people of his church and community. He would go up to individuals and read the script and message he believed God gave him. Some of his friends in the congregation thought he had become mentally unstable. Others worried a satanic spirit was deceiving him. Still others believed that God had indeed called him.[28] As Murray's art gained attention, more people from his church and community believed this experience was from God or was positive. Towards the end of his life, he was invited to lead prayer in his church, which displays a degree of acceptance by the church leadership.[29]

Approximately six months after he had his first vision at age seventy, Murray's vision turned dark when he was put in jail for a week and after that committed to Central State Mental Hospital for six weeks. He was released on 11 November 1978. The facts of his incarceration and commitment are unclear and exact information is not available because of patient confidentiality. However, an employee of Central State Mental Hospital, who wished to remain anonymous, stated that in 1978 it was possible for a family member to

---

[24]Ibid.
[25]Murray, transcript of videotaped interview.
[26]Ibid.
[27]Ibid.
[28]Pinkston interview.
[29]Ernest Ingram, telephone conversation with author, 20 July 1993.

commit someone who was a burden to take care of. The fact that Murray was only there the minimum observation time indicates he likely was not defined by the hospital staff as one who suffered from an emotional instability that would impair his ability to live a normal life.

At this time Murray was living with his son Ray and Ray's woman friend. It is not clear how they reacted to his vision and subsequent change. Murray often mentioned a woman who he believed tried to harm him and that he connected with his being taken away and locked up. One example of this is, "She know what the Lord know about her that was true. That made her go evil against me"[30] Murray believed that his vision was central in the decision to hospitalize him. He said of this experience, "They didn't understand my torment. They thought I was crazy for that but I was not. I saw [that] the Lord saw them. I was feeling all right. I was feeling like the Lord was with me and that Sunday night I had another nervous breakdown and they carried me out to the hospital."[31]

After Murray got out of the hospital, he built a separate house on the same property as the other house. He now lived alone and worked by the light of a kerosene lamp.

Communicating the Message to the World

Murray believed that God sent certain people to facilitate the communication of the message of the Holy Spirit through his art to a larger audience than the small community of Mitchell, Georgia. The Sandersville physician William Rawlings was one such person. In December 1978, one month after Murray was released from Milledgeville, he went to the office of William Rawlings. Rawlings said that Murray's initial visit related to a minor health problem.

---

[30]Murray, transcript of videotaped interview.

[31]J. B. Murray, interview with Andy Nasisse, in the catalogue for the exhibit, *Portraits from the Outside: Outsider Art—Art Brut*, Parsons School of Design Gallery, New York (Groegfeax Publishing, 1990), 78. It is not clear what Murray meant by "having another nervous breakdown." It is possible that this is how he described his visions.

About this first appointment, Rawlings elaborated: "He [Murray] decided I made him better whatever I did for him. And he decided that I had been sent from God to promulgate his message to the world. This wasn't told to me directly but was eventually what I figured out and what he admitted."[32] According to Nasisse, Murray really thought of William as "more than just a physical doctor."[33]

Murray spoke to Rawlings of "having visions, hearing voices, and receiving communications from a higher spirit that had to do with religious type things, and he had begun to implement his own form of writing." Murray began to bring Rawlings large quantities of his script and illustrations written on the backs of envelopes, in spiral notebooks, on old bills, on the covers of phone books and on anything else Murray could find. There were also long rolls of script on adding machine paper (See illustrations 5-9.). Krista Lamar, who was married to Rawlings at the time, reported that Murray would present Rawlings with numerous bundles of script on tissue paper rolled up and tied like scrolls.[34] Rawlings said that as Murray gave him the script Murray would say "Here, these things are for you. You will understand them."[35] Murray would regularly visit Rawlings's office in Sandersville (which was about thirty miles from Murray's house) without an appointment. Rawlings would always make time in his schedule to see him and receive Murray's latest script and illustrations. After a certain point, Rawlings began throwing some of Murray's work away because the closets in his office were overflowing. Murray was also at this time creating paintings and script on discarded building supplies around his house such as old stove tops, television picture tubes, and wooden paneling. (See illustrations 10-14.) Murray kept bringing so much of his script and illustrations, Rawlings finally gave him five dollars and suggested that he buy markers, drawing paper, and other materials at a local department store. He told Murray, "You know, if you're going to bring me these

[32]William Rawlings, interview with author, Sandersville GA, 1 May 1993.
[33]Nasisse, interview, 30 June 1993.
[34]Krista Lamar, telephone conversation with author, 25 February 1995.
[35]Rawlings, interview, 1 May 1993.

things, why don't you make them nice?"[36] Rawlings then described his surprise when he saw the work Murray brought him with the new materials. With the opportunity to produce on larger surfaces with art materials more conducive to creating pleasing visual effects, Murray elaborated his initial impulse, and his vision seemed to expand aesthetically. As Rawlings saw it, "[t]here was just incredible color, and an incredible sense of space and power in his work."[37] Lamar believes that Murray's compositions became more densely filled with figures when he started using poster board and larger surfaces (See illustrations 15 and 16 and color plate 2 and 3.). His first spontaneous impulses that he produced seemed to switch to an emphasis on a more careful rendering as he created on new surfaces rather than scraps of building supplies and paper. Initially the materials Murray had were not of the highest quality, (i.e. not archival). For example, Lamar and Rawlings got him poster board, crayons, watercolors, tempera and markers. Later still she and Rawlings gave Murray more professional products such as watercolor and pastel paper, oil paint sticks, and metallic and opaque markers.[38]

In the fall of 1982, Lamar took a class from Andy Nasisse, an art professor at the University of Georgia. Murray had been bringing Rawlings work for about four years, and Lamar showed Nasisse some of Murray's script and paintings. Nasisse became excited about Murray's work, and a meeting was arranged in Mitchell.[39] Murray believed that Nasisse was also being used by God as an instrument for getting Murray's message out to a larger audience. Nasisse soon began to send high quality art supplies to Murray for him to choose any that he wanted to use. According to Nasisse, he went to the art stores in Athens and bought anything he thought that Murray might like.[40]

---

[36]Ibid.
[37]Ibid.
[38]Lamar, telephone conversation.
[39]Ibid.
[40]Nasisse, interview, 18 January 1995.

Soon after Nasisse recognized the formal excellence of Murray's work, he contacted the Phyllis Kind Gallery in New York City. His idea was to introduce Murray's work in New York and then let Murray's career progress from there.[41] Phyllis Kind is a gallery owner with a history of treating artists well and with respect. Kind represents different types of artists in her gallery including academic, outsider, visionary self-taught, and folk artists. She also does not shy away from religious subject-matter, which pleased Murray. She was excited about Murray's work and decided to represent him in her gallery.[42]

Thus were forged the avenues of transporting the awareness of Murray and his art from the remote middle Georgia community to the larger world of art, which would include galleries in New York, Tokyo, and international art exhibitions and collections. Before this initial contact with Kind, however, Murray's exhibition history began in the show *Inspired Innocence*, a group show of visionary and outsider artists at Nexus Gallery in Atlanta, Georgia in 1984 His work next appeared in a group show of Black Visionaries at Indiana University, Bloomington, Indiana, with his work featured on the poster for the show *Mojo Working*, curated by Andy Nasisse. In 1986, the shows *Red Dog Running* at Ricco Johnson Gallery, New York, and a group show at the San Francisco Museum of Folk Art, curated by John Turner, included his work. In the same year Murray's work was a part of seven other group exhibitions in Pennsylvania, New York, North Carolina, Washington State, and Georgia. From 1987 till 1996 his art appeared in shows in Washington State, New York, New Jersey, Florida, and Georgia. The traveling exhibition *Parallel Visions* from the Los Angeles Museum of Art, curated by Maurice Tuchman in 1992, displayed his work, and his art was also exhibited during this time in Tokyo, Japan, at the Alpha Cubic Gallery. In the exhibit *Souls Grown Deep*, held in Atlanta, Georgia, for the 1996 Olympic games, art collector William Arnett included approximately

[41]Judith McWillie, interview with author, transcript, Athens GA, 4 April 1994.
[42]Ibid.

twenty of Murray's paintings and script displayed in a separate room within the larger show.

Despite the numerous showings and the various people from the world of art who cared about Murray's art and cared about his vision, Murray was not influenced in the core of his calling. These showings and supporters facilitated communicating Murray's own belief in what he heard and what he believed God wanted him to record. Rawlings states, "At no time did anyone tell him what to do or not do."[43] Rawlings was impressed with Murray's sincerity and strength of will in regard to his art and he suggests that Murray was profoundly honest and clear about what he wanted to accomplish:

> J. B. was one of the true individuals that I consider real. . . . There's nothing that has been created. No one told him to draw pictures because they might sell and make money, and no one told him to say this or say that because he had important visitors. That's not the way it was. He was totally sincere and very naive in his sincerity.[44]

The Psychology of Vision

Murray's mental condition at the time he was creating his art is a factor in understanding his objectives and the impetus behind his work. His brief hospitalization at Central State Mental Hospital in Milledgeville, Georgia, is likely the reason Murray has often in the past been defined as an outsider artist, a definition that focuses on an artist's mental and emotional anomaly and differences from mainstream society. If he were acting out of a state of delusion, his objectives for his art could be different than if he was responding to his conviction that he was being "called" to create his art through a teaching consistent with his faith. The question of his mental condition at the time he created his art is not an important factor for

---

[43]Rawlings, interview, 3 June 1993.
[44]Ibid.

viewing Murray's art and appreciating it formally. It is an important consideration in how one understands Murray as an artist, however. Was Murray an outsider artist, plagued by the voices of psychosis and isolated in a world of delusion? Or was he an "insider" working within a tradition, whose thinking and actions are understandable within the objectives of his spiritual world view?

An important indicator of Murray's emotional health is given by the impressions of people who knew him as a friend, family member, or artist. Most people close to Murray during the time he produced his work describe his mental and emotional state as lucid and not out of touch with reality, although they generally admit that he was unusual. During the time he knew Murray, Rawlings believed that some of Murray's thinking by conventional standards would be considered delusional, but never in the time that he knew him was he psychotic in any way nor did he have a fixation that would impair his function in society.[45]

Lamar observed Murray during the time he did his spiritual work and claimed that in a small town there are some people who are just different. "They are characters. But Murray functioned. He had a family and took care of it."[46] Nasisse described Murray as being clear thinking but with an unusual perspective that led him to consistently view the world through spiritual eyes. Nasisse added, "He was genuinely religious. I believe he really did have a window open to God. Someone with his background wouldn't, couldn't do this without a reason, a 'calling.' "[47]

Judith McWillie described her interaction with Murray as being one of sensitivity, caring, and connection between two people. As to Murray's mental or emotional state, McWillie said, "There was no way he could be a schizophrenic and be that in touch with other people." She spoke of Murray as "someone who had an open pipeline to the other side."[48] Ernest Ingram, a contemporary and a member

---

[45]Ibid.

[46]Lamar, telephone conversation.

[47]Andy Nasisse, telephone conversation with author, 5 June 1994.

[48]Judith McWillie, interview with author, Athens GA, 10 January 1995.

of Murray's church, talked also about Murray's showing people "this unusual writing that you couldn't understand."[49] Ingram mentioned that there was debate within the church he and Murray attended concerning the nature of Murray's experience.[50] Nathaniel and Larry Tucker, who lived in Mitchell and were the age of some of Murray's children, talked about how Murray came up to them around town or outside the hardware store on several occasions and started "reading" in English from a page that contained his script. Nathaniel Tucker could not remember the content of what Murray said, but it did not pertain to him (Nathaniel) personally. Concerning this "reading," Larry Tucker remarked, "He couldn't read or write yet he could read off that paper like a high school graduate."[51] In regard to Murray personally, Larry Tucker said, "He got a little out of his mind. But I reckon he was 'called'. . . ."[52]

Murray's Last Days

Towards the end of Murray's life he became aware that his work was being appreciated as art. Rawlings noted that Murray produced his script more furiously as his prostate cancer advanced. "It was like he had to complete this work before he died," Rawlings stated. McWillie remarked that Murray was also aware of people disputing over his work and was distressed about this. She added that Murray fell ill right after discovering these problems: "I don't know if it had just all run its course or if he felt sick while that was happening, but there was definitely a closure."[53]

Rawlings, McWillie, Nasisse, and Pinkston (Murray's sister-in-law) commented that the work Murray did was a source of joy and happiness for him, although the experience was not without pain

---

[49]Ernest Ingram, telephone conversation.
[50]Ibid. The people of Murray's church were not sure whether Murray's experience was from God, from a satanic spirit, or from psychological delusions.
[51]Nathaniel Tucker, interview with author, tape recording, Mitchell GA, 20 July 1993.
[52]Larry Tucker, interview with author, tape recording, Mitchell GA, 20 July 1993.
[53]McWillie, interview, 10 January 1995.

as a consequence of being misunderstood. Pinkston recounted the joy Murray would express as he told her about the art and what God told him to do and say.[54] Murray's own words reflect this attitude: "I can't need nothing else but God, like a mirror, and I'm happy. The work I'm doing, I'm happy because it's come from Him. Man couldn't do it. . . . This well is deep and never go dry."[55]

When Murray responded to his vision in 1978 while he stood in his backyard watering potatoes, he knew nothing about the end results of his obedience. He had never written nor created art before this time, and he was also not acquainted with the art establishment that would later be his primary audience and thus recipient of the message he would so fervently seek to share. He was a solitary person who believed the sun came down from the sky to illuminate not only the ground around him, but also a new path before him. Murray's response to his vision was, "Lord, I didn't know I was close enough to You for You to bless me with this gift."[56]

One wonders what the gift of J. B. Murray was and what he contributed within the world of art, a world far from rural Georgia. He presented an example of single-minded devotion to an unseen prompting. He displayed the power of purpose and belief in something larger than himself. His was a voice of compassion and courage. His was a quiet spirit, yet one with a gentle power as he requested, "Give me a louder word up."

---

[54]Pinkston, interview.
[55]Murray, published interview, 79.
[56]Murray, transcript of videotaped interview.

1. J. B. Murray in his yard in Mitchell, Georgia, 1985 (Photograph by Andy Nasisse).

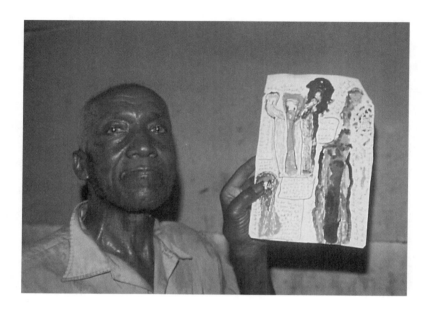

2. J. B. Murray, 1982 (Photograph taken by Andy Nasisse on the day he met Murray in Mitchell, Georgia).

3. Murray's house in Mitchell, Georgia, 1985 (Photograph by Andy Nasisse).

4. The well in Murray's yard in Mitchell, GA, where he filled the jar of water through which he viewed his art, 1985 (Photograph by Judith McWillie).

5. William Rawlings's drawer showing Murray's early script on envelopes and scraps of paper (Photograph by Fred Padgelek at the home of William Rawlings, Sandersville, Georgia, 1993).

6. A spiral notebook Murray completely filled with script drawn in red marker, 12" x 12", ca. 1978-1980 (Photograph by Fred Padgelek at the home of William Rawlings, Sandersville, Georgia, 1993).

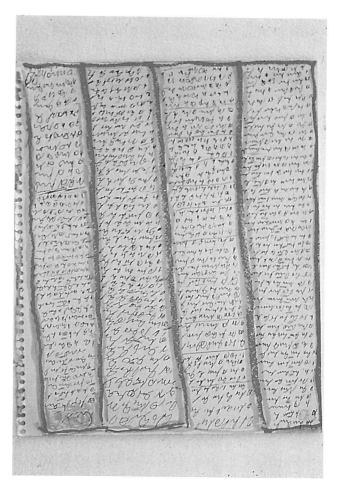

7. Ink and crayon on paper, 8" x 11", ca. 1978-1986 (Photograph by Andy Nasisse).

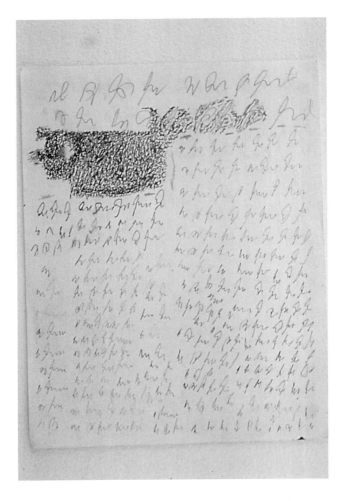

8. Ink on paper, 8" x 11", ca. 1978-1985
(Photograph by Judith McWillie).

9. Marker on adding machine tape, 1978
(Photograph by Fred Padgelek at the home of
William Rawlings, Sandersville, Georgia).

10. Tempera and marker on a stove top, 24" x 24", ca. 1978 (Photograph by Judith McWillie).

11. Tempera and marker on TV picture tube, 25" x 20", ca. 1978 (Photograph by Judith McWillie).

12. Wallboard, tempera, and marker, 18" x 24",
ca. 1978 (Photograph by Judith McWillie).

13. Marker on wooden wall panels and paper (on right), approximately 12" x 48" each, ca. 1978-1982 (Photograph by Andy Nasisse).

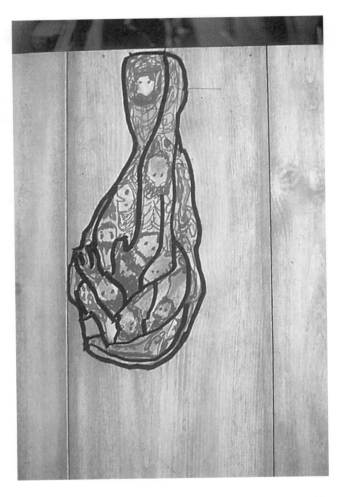

14. Marker on wooden wall paneling, 24" x 48",
ca. 1978-1980 (Photograph by Judith McWillie).

15. Marker on poster board, 28" x 22", ca. 1980-1982 (Photograph by Andy Nasisse).

16. Marker on poster board, 28" x 22", ca. 1980-1982
(Photograph by Andy Nasisse).

17. Marker and watercolor on paper, 24" x 18", ca. 1985-1986 (Photograph by Andy Nasisse).

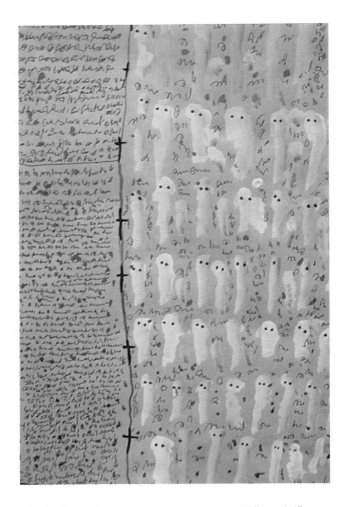

18. Ink and tempera on paper, 11" x 14", ca. 1982-1986 (Photograph by Andy Nasisse).

19. Marker and watercolor on paper, 18" x 24", ca. 1982-1986 (Photograph by Fred Padgelek, taken at the Berman Gallery, Atlanta, Georgia).

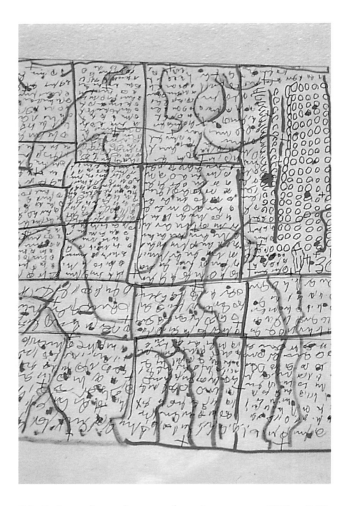

20. Ink and marker on drawing paper, 22" x 24",
ca. 1982-1986 (Photograph by Andy Nasisse).

21. Ink and watercolor on paper, 24" x 30", ca. 1982-1986 (Photograph by Fred Padgelek at the home of William Rawlings, Sandersville, Georgia).

22. Ink and watercolor on paper, 18" x 24", ca. 1982-1986 (Photograph by Andy Nasisse).

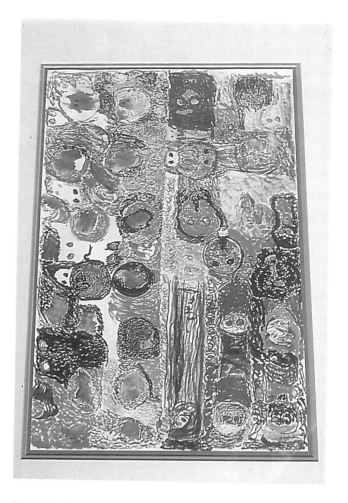

23. Marker on paper, 18" x 24", ca. 1982-1986 (Photograph by Fred Padgelek at the home of William Rawlings, Sandersville, Georgia).

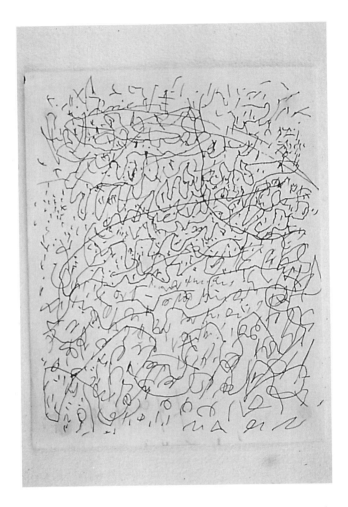

24. Ink on paper, 8" x 11", ca. 1978 (Photograph by Judith McWillie).

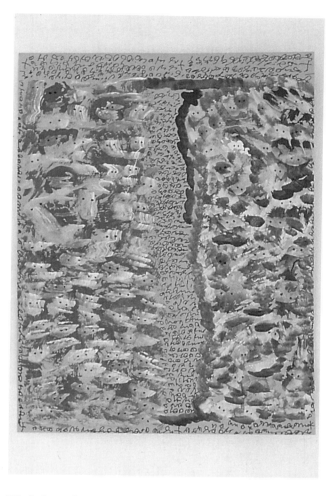

25. Ink and tempera on pink paper, 18" x 24", ca. 1987 (Photograph from the Phyllis Kind Gallery, New York, New York).

26. Ink and watercolor on pink paper, 10" x 14 1/3", ca. 1987 (Photograph by Andy Nasisse).

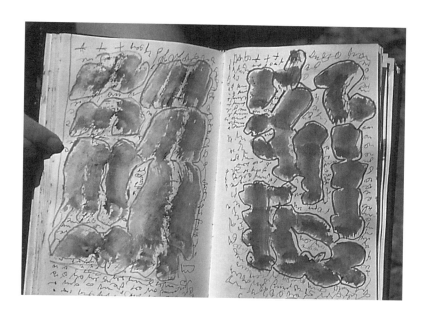

27. Two pages in the middle of Murray's last sketch book, 5"
x 8" each, ca. 1987 (Photograph by Fred Padgelek at the
home of William Rawlings, Sandersville, Georgia).

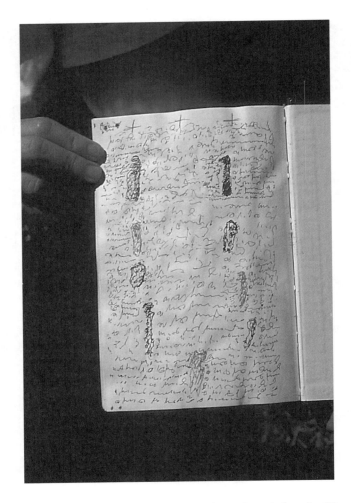

28. The last page in Murray's last sketch book, 5"
x 8" each, ca. 1987 (Photograph by Fred Padgelek
at the home of William Rawlings, Sandersville,
Georgia).

29. Silver metallic marker and watercolor on paper, 18" x 22", ca. 1987 (Photograph by Andy Nasisse).

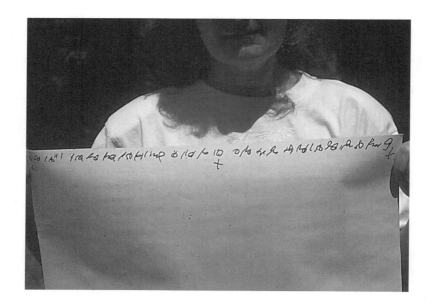

30. Script on the back of one of Murray's paintings. His "signature."(Photograph by Fred Padgelek at the home of William Rawlings, Sandersville, Georgia)

3

OUT OF THE DARKNESS
SHALL COME THE LIGHT;
OUT OF SILENCE, DANCING[1]:
SPIRITUAL INFLUENCES IN RURAL MIDDLE
GEORGIA AND MURRAY'S ART

The South of the 1930s and 1940s largely shaped Murray. Beneath the complex social structure of the rural South, with its history of slavery, Jim Crow segregation, racial violence, and initially slow economic recovery after the Civil War, exists the powerful presence of religion.[2] The southern region of the United States, which consists of a juxtaposition of African, European, and Native American spiritual beliefs, creates a creolized culture that emerges from diverse origins and forms a rich background with powerful spiritual and emotional forces.[3]

Although the primary impetus behind Murray's art was his evangelical Christian faith, in Murray's rural, middle Georgia the mixture of West African and Southern American spiritual influences formed a unique hybrid. This area displayed stronger West African spiritual characteristics than other sections of the country due to African spiritual perspectives brought to the South through the Atlantic slave trade. [4]

---

[1]T. S. Eliot, from *The Four Quartets*.

[2]Alice Rae Yelen, *Passionate Visions of the American South* (New Orleans: New Orleans Museum of Art, 1993), 45.

[3]Ibid.

[4]Judith McWillie, "Another Face of the Diamond: Black Traditional Art from the Deep South," *The Clarion* (Fall 1987): 42.

The Southern evangelical Protestant faith, especially within the African-American church, includes a more experiential, ritualistic interpretation of the faith than does a European-American understanding or a northern African-American perspective. From the influence of West African spirituality, there is a belief in the constant presence of good and evil forces. There is also a greater reliance on ritual to control the unseen forces that surround us. Murray's development of a ritual of looking through the water as a part of the presentation and spirituality of his art, is likely the result of West African influences upon his understanding of the faith.

West African Influences

Although the direct importation of Africans sold into slavery was banned in 1808, importation persisted illegally after this date for economic reasons, and Africans continued to arrive along the southern Atlantic coast. These Africans were predominantly from the Angolan region of West Central Africa near the Kongo River.[5] During this period of direct importation, West African languages, religion, and philosophy entered the American South without any dilution. African-American society in areas of the Deep South developed uniquely out of the combination of this strong infusion from West Africa into the southeastern United States.[6]

Most Africans who came over in the slave trade held indigenous, traditional African beliefs even though Islam, and to a lesser extent Christianity, had extended into sub-Saharan Africa.[7] Western Africa sustained a predominantly polytheistic form of religion where there existed many and varied smaller gods. Many of these deities represented the forces of nature. The people sought to propitiate moods of destruction and elicit good will through ritual and ceremony.[8] Nearly all West Africans had a conception of an omnipotent, ubiquitous

---

[5]Ibid.
[6]Ibid.
[7]Albert S. Raboteau, *A Fire in the Bones* (Boston: Beacon Press, 1995), 7.
[8]E. G. Parrinder, *African Traditional Religion* (London: Sheldon Press, 1974), 24.

Supreme Being. This God was higher than the local gods and higher than deceased ancestors and other spirits that the people interacted with and prayed to daily. In times of great need and tragedy, the West Africans understood this great God could be approached directly without a mediator so that prayers could be answered.[9] This tradition relates to Murray's understanding of God within evangelical Christianity. Murray frequently called upon Jesus in his daily struggles as the aspect of God he could contact directly and one to whom he could feel close. He claimed, "Jesus, you are my only friend."[10] As is characteristic of evangelical Christianity, he believed Jesus existed as the mediator between the Christian and God the Father. The African understanding of a larger and more powerful, albeit remote God, combined with accessible deities, is similar in concept.

The West African conception of the power and presence of ancestors has some definite links to Murray's spiritual understanding as indicated by his vision of his dead mother beseeching God on his behalf. In this spiritual experience, Murray believed he heard his mother's voice talking to God. Murray's vision of his mother echoes West African religious teaching that proclaims that ancestors who cross over to the realm beyond this life are available to help and guide the living. These ancestors are conceived to have the weaknesses of human beings and often need appeasing so that their jealousy or irritability does not cause harm. In an invisible realm, they can remain near the living without the living being aware of their presence. Also, somewhat similar is the belief common among the people of East and West Africa of spiritual guides that guard and protect. In African Traditional Religion there existed the concept that the spirit guide gave both good and bad fortune, and constituted the fate of the individual.[11] This spirit offered advice as an inner voice of conscience or, if angered, could cause harm.

---

[9]Ibid., 42.

[10]Transcript (in author's possession) of J. B. Murray, interview with Judith McWillie, video recording, Mitchell GA, 31 May 1985.

[11]Parrinder, *African Traditional Religion*, 136.

Murray believed in the presence of good and evil forces that controlled much of everyday life. The perception of a natural world controlled by spirits relates to "conjure" or "hoodoo," a concept common within the enslaved African-American population which had strong West African connections. A tradition of folk conviction and practice, conjure is believed by some to give the power of the supernatural over everyday circumstances. Conjure remains strong among African-Americans in rural middle Georgia where Murray grew up, and also comprised a vital part of Murray's understanding. In West Africa, and among some African-Americans today, unexplained sickness or misfortune is often assumed to be caused by another's hand—an enemy's. The enslaved African-Americans often believed that adversity resided not in blind fate or chance but the ill will of someone working through a conjurer. This belief in the power of a foe can explain the mystery of evil and undeserved misfortune. Conjure can give a sense of power and control in a spiritual realm where little power and control exists over temporal circumstances. African-Americans generally think of conjure, or hoodoo, as their own separate tradition. Whites can be afraid of conjure, but whites are almost never conjurers. Because it conflicts with Christianity's providence of God, according to many white believers, conjure is mostly relegated to the devil and satanic powers.[12] Few ministers conjure. But even though some consider conjuring to be immoral, many African-Americans consider it foolish to deny its power. Believing that the boundaries of this world are easily crossed by spirits, many rural Georgia African-Americans still need to find a way to remain open to visits from dead relatives, yet obtain protection from hostile influences. They keenly believe in the presence of both good and evil forces, and often they commission root doctors, charms, and prayers for good fortune and protection.[13]

---

[12]Raboteau, *A Fire in the Bones*, 284.

[13]Donald G. Matthews, *Religion in the Old South* (Chicago and London: The University of Chicago Press, 1977), 210.

Murray spoke often of people putting a "root" on him, and also of harm being done to him by someone using a poison made from butterfly wings that made him sick. His speech was replete with references to conjure, hoodoo, and the power of enemies.[14] Although he respected the power of conjure, he expressed that his spirit-art and the ritual he performed around this were Christian and not hoodoo and that "Jesus is stronger than hoodoo."[15] In his evangelical Christian understanding he believed hoodoo was satanic. Conjure and hoodoo constituted spiritual entities he fearfully respected but did not practice himself. Murray often called on Jesus to protect him from the conjure of those he believed wished him harm.[16]

Conjure is different from the common understanding of spiritual forces within evangelical Christianity. In contrast to the West African concept of ancestral guidance, Christianity's Holy Spirit consists of God in the form of a beneficent spirit. A believer seeks to please God through obedience to the teachings and precepts of the Bible; however, there is no appeasing, except for a believer's seeking forgiveness of his/her sins in order to restore a closeness of relationship to God. Spirits within evangelical understanding are either from God or from Satan. Evil spirits cannot do good, though they can disguise themselves as angels of light initially,[17] and the spirits of God cannot do evil.

Murray's belief in the Holy Spirit moving his hand possibly indicates a mixture of West African and evangelical Protestant understanding. West African Traditional Religion is replete with ritualistic ceremonies that have the specific objective of evoking aid, protection, or guidance from a spiritual dimension. Spiritual possession constitutes an example of such metaphysical intervention and was central to the traditional religion of the West African people. Here believers beseeched the gods to come down to earth and "ride" a person, putting him or her in a state of possession. Many rituals and

---

[14]Murray, transcript of videotaped interview.
[15]Ibid.
[16]Ibid.
[17]2 Corinthians 11:14.

ceremonies of the West Africans sought to evoke the supernatural by gradually enticing a spirit into an attractive environment. When a spirit descended upon a person, he or she took on the personality of the spirit in body movement, facial expressions, and speech.[18] A vital difference between the evangelical Protestant belief in guidance from the Holy Spirit and the West African ritual of spiritual possession is that in the former the Holy Spirit does not take over a person's personality. The personality remains intact, while the words a person speaks reveal the wisdom of God. The Holy Spirit is God as the third person of the Trinity and is described in the Bible as the Comforter and Spirit of Truth.[19] Murray's repeated request for God to give him a "louder word up" to ascertain whether his words pleased God indicates his evangelical Protestant understanding of the guidance of the Holy Spirit more than the West African concept of spiritual possession.

Possible Influence of African-Islam and Murray's Script

The creation of Murray's script might be the result of an African Islamic way of understanding the written word. Since the Bible does not mention the spiritual gift of a person writing in an esoteric script literally produced by the Holy Spirit moving the person's hand, this fact raises the possibility of Muslim influence in middle Georgia, which historically connects the execution of certain script with religious devotion, prayer, and empowerment from God.

Based on the documented presence of African Muslims who were brought over in the Atlantic slave trade, an Islamic spiritual influence possibly exists in rural middle Georgia. How many Muslims came into antebellum America within the Atlantic slave trade is difficult to know. Philip Curtin's book, *Economic Change in Pre-Colonial Africa*, suggests that while approximately 29,695 African Muslims arrived in this country, their influence often exceeds actual numbers. A number

---

[18]Raboteau, *A Fire in the Bones*, 59.
[19]John 14:16-17.

of accounts of enslaved African-American Muslims who had memorized the entire Koran in an effort to keep their Islamic faith vital and pass it on to others, particularly their children, are extant.[20]

Beyond the fact that Murray's script was a product of his reverence for the authority of the Bible, stemming from his evangelical understanding and perhaps his visual impression of seeing the Bible, the production of his mystic writing might be the result of a uniquely Islamic way of understanding the written word.

Murray's art and some beliefs within African Islam have striking similarities within the form, objectives, and ritual. For instance, Murray's first work consisted of his script. Within Islam, the act of writing presents a special act of devotion, whereas writing itself is not special and linked to devotion within Christianity. Historically, to the enslaved African-American Muslim, the act of writing in Arabic was closely akin to believing and worshiping.[21] This practice set persons apart as important members of a community because they often acted as spiritual counselors through this prayerful script in Africa and later in America. In Islam, writing often gives authority believed to be from Allah.[22]

---

[20]C. Eric. Lincoln, "The American Muslim Mission in the Context of American Social History," in The Muslim Community in North America, Earle H. Waugh, Baha Abu-Laban and Regula B. Queshi, eds. (Edmonton: The University of Alberta Press, 1983) 218. A slaveholder named Bryan Edwards gives an account of an enslaved Mandingo servant, also in the South, who could write in Arabic. In 1805, an account also existed of an enslaved African-American named Sambo (probably originally Samba) who ran away with three other "new Negroes." Sambo also wrote in the Arabic language. Nero, another enslaved African American, was customarily given beef instead of pork for his meat ration on a South Carolina plantation in the 1840s. This dietary request presumably was because of the Muslim restriction against eating pork; and one can assume that Nero was Muslim. Others, (Omar, Abu Bakr, and Rahahman, for example) wrote Arabic after being separated from Africa for more than thirty years. It is obvious that these enslaved African-Americans practiced aspects of their Muslim faith and did not forget the Islamic lessons from West Africa when they arrived in the South.

[21]Allan D. Austin, African Muslims in Ante-bellum America—A Source book (New York and London: Garland Publishing, Inc., 1984), 17.

[22]Ronald A. T. Judy, (Dis) Forming the American Canon—African-Arabic Slave Narratives and the Vernacular (Minneapolis: The University of Minnesota Press, 1993), 173.

The fact that Murray handed out his script in sealed envelopes could relate to the African-Islamic custom of using script in their ceremonies and art forms to secure Allah's protection and blessing. For instance, an amulet is an African-Islamic charm ceremoniously created and worn by a person seeking Allah's favor and power. The amulet, secret from everyone but the person and the counselor, consists of concealed truths and is almost always shielded from the public eye and kept in the shadows of the culture.[23] The African Islamic amulets, regardless of their form or purpose, most often consist of two parts—a written portion and a design or graphic element. The written part originates from the various Islamic sources including the Koran, astrological treatises, divination manuals, or books on numerology. The design part may consist of magical squares, images of the planets and their movements, or various geometric configurations.[24] Thus the words and pictures comprise the essence of these secret charms. The writing, often executed in alternating directions, is commonly divided into different sections and categories. The words are scattered among geometric figures and are arranged in squares or broken down into letters, much as in examples of Murray's work. (See illustrations 3, 20, 21, and 24-29.)

Another connection with Islam may exist in Murray's custom of looking at his art and interpreting it through a jar of water. One Islamic tradition involves a special vial worn as an amulet used by a Mamadou, an Islamic spiritual counselor. This vial contains a special solution called nassa-ji, a substance used for protection and receiving the favor of Allah. The liquid consists of a solution made from the washing of the words and marks placed on a Koranic board into a jar or container worn in secrecy. Worshipers believe that the dissolved Koranic words bestow power to the person wearing the amulet. Such an amulet is created within a ritual that involves the Mamadou giving counsel to the person, presumably from the words of the Koran

---

[23]René A. Bravmann, *African Islam* (Washington DC: The Smithsonian Institute Press; London and Great Britain: Ethnographica Ltd., 1983), 37.
[24]Ibid.

written on the Koranic board. Many other similar charms were generally written on paper, soaked in water and then applied by their new owners as a special solution to protect against attacks of witches and to bring good fortune.

Some similarities exist between the creation of these amulets and the art and ritual of J. B. Murray. These similarities include utilizing words and drawings in a sectional pattern, handwriting going in different directions, the application of an esoteric script, incorporating water in the ceremony as an element in an empowerment process, and the role of the Mamadou as a spiritual counselor. Similarities also exist in the ritual of the creation and use of the amulet within practices where the Arabic words express power as the language of Allah, and Murray's belief that the script he put on the surface before him communicated a message from the Holy Spirit. In both the amulet and in Murray's production of his script and drawing, the words shared God's wisdom through the person performing the writing and drawing. Like the African Islamic amulet that consists of two parts, the words and a design or graphic element, Murray's art often included both words and abstract designs or figures. Different parts made up the experience for Murray as he went through the process of the writing, drawing and painting, and looking through the jar of water while he counseled a visitor. Similarly, the African Islamic creator of the amulet went through a ritual to produce the amulet and give it meaning. Therefore, although not confirmed specifically by tangible evidence of Muslim input in Mitchell, Georgia, an Afri-can-Islamic influence could have been a factor in the form of Murray's compositions and his ritual.

Writing in a mysterious script has occurred in the work of other Southern visionary self-taught artists. Some examples include Minnie Evans, who used "signing" as an embellishment in her drawings; Lonnie Holley, who painted the ceiling of his house with abstract ciphers; Leroy Person, who carved script into wooden panels, Joe Light, who wrote "Abraham's writing" on wooden plaques and placed them in his yard for all to see, and James Hampton who filled notebooks he called "St. James Revelations" with cryptic words he believed Jesus gave him at night to instruct him on his art. In Kongo rituals there also exists a spirit script that presents messages from another world that in some way would be interpreted, just as the glossolalia in the New Testament is presumed to have an interpreter.[25] It is difficult to determine the origin of this practice of cryptic writing believed to originate from God, but both Murray and James Hampton, for instance, recorded the script in notebooks and considered the writing part of the instruction for their call. A friend of Hampton's asked many times about the content of his vision and the writing, and Hampton would always say, "Christ appeared at the corner of the alley, standing in the light," and told him what to do.[26]

The faith that apparently propelled Murray's art was likely a hybrid of both West African and Protestant Christian beliefs. Certain forms within his art, his ritual, and his "writing in the spirit" relate to various aspects of a West African view of the spiritual cosmos. However, Murray transformed these West African influences into his overarching evangelical Christian understanding of being "called" by God to work for the salvation of lost souls.

Evangelical Christianity

Evangelical Christianity, the faith Murray grew up with and was taught all his life through his attendance at a Baptist church, is a faith that is difficult to define precisely because of the diversity included within this broad term. The theology of evangelical Christianity can range from extreme conservatism, as in fundamentalism, to a liberal position that allows for a more non-literal interpretive approach to the Bible. Evangelicalism consists of four main branches: classical,

---

[25]Ibid., 113.
[26]James L. Foy and James P. McMurrer, "James Hampton, Artist and Visionary," *Transcultural Aspects of Psychiatric Art*, vol. 4 of Psychiatry and Art series, Irene Jakab, ed. (New York: Karger and Bisel, 1975), 720.

pietistic, fundamentalist, and progressive.[27] Classical evangelicals adhere to the main doctrines and beliefs of the Protestant Reformation. These doctrines include the ultimate authority of the Bible, justification by faith, and a substitutionary view of the atonement.[28] Classical evangelicals tend to emphasize the creeds of the faith over religious experience. Pietistic evangelicals also adhere to the doctrines of the Protestant Reformation, but they incorporate the experiential emphasis of pietism, Puritanism, and the evangelical awakenings or revivals of the eighteenth century.[29] Basically, their theology is similar to the Reformation, but, unlike the classical evangelicals, they stress conversion and holy living, revivals, social reform, and "higher life" movements where the believer's objective is to forge a deeper spiritual understanding and connection with God. The fundamentalist evangelicals are defined by many of the doctrines of classical and pietistic evangelism, but focus on a few "fundamental" beliefs that are in direct opposition to "liberal, critical and evolutionary thinking."[30]

---

[27]Timothy P. Weber, "Premillennialism and the Branches of Evangelism," in *The Variety of American Evangelicalism*, Donald Dayton and Robert K. Johnson, eds. (Knoxville: University of Tennessee Press, 1991), 12.

[28]Ibid. The *ultimate authority of the Bible* refers to the belief that God inspired the Bible through the words of the biblical authors and therefore it is true and has His authority. *Justification by faith* means that one is acceptable to God through his or her faith in Christ. The *substitutionary view of the atonement* means that Christ's death on the cross substituted for believer's sins thus providing salvation for those who trust in Christ.

[29]Ibid., 13. *The Great Awakenings*, or *Great Revivals* were a series of outpourings of spiritual renewal and fervor that seemed to sweep over different parts of the Christian world. This happened in the southern United States between 1800 and 1805 and is often termed the Second Great Awakening. However, this was the first time such a sweeping revival had happened in the South. The First Great Awakening in America was one north of Maryland in 1739-1750. A "great awakening" needs certain conditions to support it such as a connection between various churches and ministers and a core group of fervent believers who perceive that society is in spiritual decline and needs God's intervention. These conditions were not characteristic of the South before the late 1790s. The Great Awakening brought in a more informal, experiential form of Protestantism not present in the formal style of the Anglican Church of the South. It was this change that most affected the enslaved African-Americans and made Christianity a faith they embraced and made their own. Southern society would ultimately be transformed by this interpretation of Christianity. *Encyclopedia of Religion in the South*, Samuel S. Hill, ed. (Macon GA: Mercer University Press, 1984), 311.

[30]Ibid.

According to George M. Marsden, fundamentalism's primary distinction embraces a militancy in its approach to the faith: a belief that Christians should not mix excessively with non-Christians except to convert them, a belief that the Bible is inerrant and should be taken literally whenever possible, and a belief that the historical study of the Bible attacks its authority and has destroyed liberal churches and rendered them useless and without God's power. Most fundamentalists believe they are in a battle between good and evil and they conduct themselves as warriors. Not all evangelicals are fundamentalists, but all fundamentalists tend to be evangelical.[31] Progressive evangelicals incorporate beliefs from the other groups; however, they do this with a deliberate contemporary stance. Most seek to hold on to the foundational beliefs of the faith, yet adjust certain doctrines in the line of modern thought and ideas. Their parameters tend to be less fixed, but basically they possess a traditional orthodoxy with less emphasis on biblical inerrancy, incorporate biblical criticism, and believe certain teachings in the Bible can be altered to support contemporary ideas.

Murray's Christian beliefs are a combination of both a fundamentalist understanding of evangelical Protestantism, and a pietistic approach. His fundamentalist understanding is apparent by his

---

[31]George M. Marsden, "Fundamentalism and American Evangelicalism," in *The Variety of American Evangelicalism*, Donald Dayton and Robert K. Johnson, eds. (Knoxville: The University of Tennessee Press, 1991) 22. There is a contemporary trend within a number of mainstream Protestant denominations for splinter groups to form comprised of believers who desire a spiritual depth they believe has been lost in churches that do not respect the Bible as the word of God. These new denominations believe the Bible is inerrant. They have similarities to fundamentalists but there are distinct differences. There is not the emphasis on the rules of the faith, (except those actually stated in the Bible), but on a personal relationship with God through Christ. There is also not the tendency to isolate from the unbelieving world, but to freely interact with the idea of sharing Christ through one's life, words, and deeds. There is a respect for truth wherever and through whomever it might be presented; thus philosophy and ideas that fit with God's truth as revealed in the Bible are as acceptable as what is written by other believers. These congregations tend to be middle-class to affluent, and well educated. One such denomination is the Presbyterian Church of America (PCA) that split from the Presbyterian, USA, because they believed the denomination was losing its power, effectiveness, and connection to God as its views conformed to the world and not the Bible.

emphasis on the foundational Christian imperative on salvation, a belief in an ever-present struggle between good and evil, as illustrated by his own words,[32] and his respect for the Bible and its authority. His pietistic understanding is shown by his acceptance of ecstatic spiritual gifts such as visions and voices and his belief that the Holy Spirit actually was moving his hand to create his art.

The Historic Roots of Evangelicalism

Historically, the evangelical Protestant perception of Christianity to which Murray responded so strongly arose in part as a reaction against religious laxity and the theological naturalism of the eighteenth century in Great Britain and British America. Some studies begin the evangelical movement with the Second Great Awakening and rapid denominational growth on the American frontier.[33] The Great Awakenings or revivals swept over most of the British North American colonies in the 1740s and swept intermittently into the South during the 1780s and 1790s. Various scholars of religion believe that these revivals or "awakenings" started the evangelical movement in America. Other scholars believe that evangelicalism involves a continuation of European originated reformation themes such as the authority of Scripture and salvation by grace through faith.[34] Whatever the exact origins, however, evangelicalism was and is a dynamic social phenomenon responsible for shaping a unique consciousness. By the early decades of the nineteenth century, evangelicalism became a dominant religious power.[35] Its goals

---

[32]Chapter 1 includes Murray's words from interviews with McWillie that demonstrate both his emphasis upon salvation and his concept of a battle between good and evil being waged daily.

[33]Leonard I. Sweet, "The Evangelical Tradition in America," in *The Evangelical Tradition in America*, Leonard I. Sweet, ed. (Macon GA: Mercer University Press, 1984), 3.

[34]Ibid. *Salvation by grace through faith* means one receives salvation through faith in Jesus Christ, not through earning heaven through doing good deeds. (Ephesians 2:8)

[35]Albert J. Raboteau, "The Black Experience in American Evangelicalism: The Meaning of Slavery," in *The Evangelical Tradition in America*, Leonard I. Sweet, ed. (Macon GA: Mercer University Press, 1995), 182.

consisted of the reformation of society; it did not keep within the bounds of religion. This social dimension constituted a vital part of the evangelical vision of seeking and saving the lost and extricating evil and moral decay from within the individual and ultimately from the larger society.[36] It could at times present a very united front for change as it sought to make America a nation under God.

The rise of slavery greatly affected evangelical Protestantism in the southern colonies. It essentially introduced into southern Evangelicalism a pathological aspect to the faith in which religious ideals of love and charity in social relationships were radically re-interpreted to justify slavery.[37] The Christian ideals of equality were pushed aside as economic concerns dominated. As the enslaved African-Americans witnessed the hypocrisy, inequality, and brutality at the core of the slaveholder's religion, they struggled to differentiate their faith from this example and find their own comprehension of Christianity.

African-American Culture and Evangelicalism

Because Murray was African-American, it is important to examine some of the distinctions found within African-American evangelical Protestantism and the origins of these differences in order to reveal possible influences upon Murray's particular comprehension of the Christian faith. For instance, in seeking to discover their voice and unique perception, the enslaved African-Americans emphasized aspects of the evangelical Christian faith different than what the slaveholders emphasized. These differences include a reaction to the specific state of enslavement and a distinct style of worship that emphasized the experiential aspects of the faith rather than reading and studying the Bible.

---

[36]Sweet, "The Evangelical Tradition in America," 34.

[37]Jon Butler, "Enlarging the Bonds of Christ: Slavery, Evangelism, and the Christianization of the White South, 1690-1790," in The Evangelical Tradition in America, Leonard I. Sweet, ed. (Macon GA: Mercer University Press, 1984), 107.

The former difference concerns the issue of freedom. Slavery involved a way of life that had a psychological effect that no one who had not experienced being enslaved could wholly understand. Because of this state of bondage, the enslaved strongly linked the providence of God to their eventual liberation and forged a theology that emphasized freedom. These African-Americans commonly believed that God worked throughout history to free captives, both spiritually and physically. They often directly identified with the children of Israel who were captive in Egypt, and their prayers habitually centered on the ability to cope until bondage ended. Many African-Americans within slavery postulated that the end of bondage rested in God's hands but that God used humans as instruments to bring about His will.[38] Consequently, the African-American's prayers and spiritual songs often indicated a longing for a person like Moses to guide them to freedom.[39]

The evangelical faith of the enslaved African-Americans commonly focused on the experience of God's Spirit and states of ecstatic possession as the core of the Christian faith. White and northern African-American missionaries, who placed less emphasis on experiential aspects in their understanding of the faith, were shocked to discover that other African-Americans considered the direct encountering of God as the norm of Christianity and valued this type of occurrence over reading and studying the biblical teachings and principles. Some scholars have theorized that the African heritage that had placed spirit possession at the core of religious worship had influenced the enslaved African-Americans' interpretation of Christianity.[40] The African-Americans within the confines of slavery, however, often associated reading the Bible with the slaveholders' version of Christianity that they believed was not as authentic as their own more ecstatic experiences of hearing about the teachings of the

---

[38]Raboteau, "The Black Experience in American Evangelicalism," 190.

[39]Milton C. Sernett, *Afro-American Religious History: A Documentary Witness* (Durham NC: Duke University Press, 1985), 137.

[40]Raboteau, "The Black Experience in American Evangelicalism," 189.

Bible in dreams and visions. Yet they revered the Bible as a sacred book and exalted it as an outward symbol of the faith.

In the late eighteenth century African-Americans, both enslaved and free, Southern and Northern, began to convert to Christianity in large numbers. By 1800 the African-American church, whether with enslaved or free parishioners, had begun. By 1830, a new generation of African-American clergymen had developed in response to the congregationalist government of the evangelical church, which allowed anyone "led by the Spirit" to take part in the worship service. This meant that the African-Americans were no longer dependent upon white pastors for hearing the Christian message.[41]

Singing, dancing, and shouting were central to the African-American evangelical Protestant faith in the South. This contrasted to the African-American evangelical churches in the Northern states that had more of an emphasis on rules, duties, obligations, and education. Some Northerners disdained the degree of experiential and ecstatic aspects of the faith in the South. An example is a Northern African-American missionary named Daniel Alexander Payne, who began working among freemen. Payne disliked, for example, former enslaved African-American's "ring-shout," which he ridiculed as a "voo-doo dance, heathenish, and a disgrace to the race."[42] He was surprised to discover the resiliency of this custom. To the former enslaved African-Americans of the South, the ring-shout often constituted the essence of their cultural identity.[43] In both the Southern and Northern African-American evangelical churches, the white fundamentalists' preoccupation with the question of biblical inerrancy never was as dogmatically defended as it was in the South. While African-American Christians appealed to biblical authority, they subordinated the adamant stance of literalism to spiritual

---

[41]Ibid., 182.
[42]Ibid., 192. The "ring-shout" is a dance where the participants circle counterclock-wise and shout out as the Spirit moves them. This is an example of the encouragement of spontaneous expressions of spiritual impulses.
[43]Ibid.

expressiveness. Their approach was often more intuitive and flexible in relation to biblical interpretation.

Contemporary Evangelicalism

For both blacks and whites there came a time in America when old religious orthodoxy waned for a vast number of people. The once dominant traditional religious viewpoint was often eclipsed by the skepticism of modern empirical thinking. Many historians date this change beginning in the 1890s. The traditional religious viewpoint further diminished with a disillusionment many people experienced after World War II. By 1980, regardless of when the trend began, polls showed that sixty-one million Americans did not attend church and that conventional Christian views were being seriously questioned.[44] Most of the mainline denominations and the Roman Catholic church had lost millions of parishioners, and the decline in membership continued. As the end of the century neared, the future of organized religion in America as we know it seemed uncertain.

In 1980, however, it became apparent that there existed a movement churning below the surface that eventually burst forth into American awareness after years of the evangelical impulse remaining hidden. Again, the evangelical Protestant movement affected the country. The year 1976 was defined as the year of the Evangelical by both *Time* and *Newsweek* magazines. Suddenly, the general public was again aware of the existence of this religious influence.[45] In 1976 Eldridge Cleaver, the leader of the Black Panthers, announced he had become a born-again Christian; Charles Colson's autobiography *Born Again* constantly appeared on the best-seller list, and a Southern Baptist, Jimmy Carter, became president of the United States. By 1980 at least thirty million Americans considered themselves reborn

---

[44]Sernett, *Afro-American Religious History*, 142.

[45]Grant Wacker, "Searching for Norman Rockwell: Popular Evangelism in Contemporary America," in *The Evangelical Tradition in America*, Leonard I. Sweet, ed. (Macon GA: Mercer University Press, 1984), 291.

evangelical Christians and another twenty million claimed evangelical beliefs and sympathy.[46]

After almost a century of quiet, there exists little consensus as to why evangelicals so forcefully erupted again into America's religious awareness. The cause could have been a reaction against the rationalism of this technological age, or perhaps the popularity of evangelicalism was due to the fact that the evangelical churches asked something of the believers and had a definite structure that people longed for in a time of permissiveness. The financial success of certain parts of the movement that allowed them to promote their views by television could have enabled their message to become ensconced in the consciousness of the country. Evangelicalism came to affect all denominations and was a movement not merely for the poor and disenfranchised; this movement impacted on all socio-economic, racial, and ethnic groups as a wider variety of people shared in the evangelical impulse in America.[47]

The Response of Murray's Church to His Experience

Starting in 1978, when Murray experienced his first vision and began creating his art, a number of members within his Baptist church questioned the origins of his vision. According to their understanding, Murray's experience could be from God, or from Murray's own delusions, or from the satanic realm of false prophecy. Followers of evangelical Protestantism believe in both good and evil forces in the universe. An ecstatic phenomenon does not in itself give proof of being spoken to or called by God. Both the godly and false prophets can perform miracles.[48] One of the primary tests of a prophet whom God calls, as understood within evangelical Protestantism, concerns godly "fruit" in the person's life. True prophets will exhibit a lifestyle that conforms to biblical principles of high morality and embodies the

---

[46]Ibid.
[47]Ibid., 292.
[48]Ibid., 293.

Color Plate 1. Murray standing beside an early painting of tempera and marker on wallboard, 18" x 24", ca. 1978-1980. Also shown is Murray's script on boards in the background (Photograph by Andy Nasisse).

Color Plate 2. Marker on poster board, 28" x 22", ca. 1980-1982 (Photograph by Andy Nasisse).

Color Plate 3. Marker on poster board, 28" x 22", ca. 1980-1982 (Photograph by Andy Nasisse).

Color Plate 4. Watercolor and marker on paper, 20" x 22", ca. 1982-1986 (Photograph by Andy Nasisse).

Color Plate 5. Marker and tempera on blue paper, 18" x 24", ca. 1986 (Photograph by Andy Nasisse).

Color Plate 6a. Metallic marker, ink, and tempera on rose paper, 18" x 24", ca. 1985-1986 (Photograph from the Phyllis Kind Gallery, New York City, New York).

Color Plate 6b. Metallic and opaque marker and water-color, 22" x 28", ca. 1985 (Photograph by Fred Padgelek at the home of William Rawlings, Sanders-sville, Georgia).

Color Plate 7. Oil pastel, marker, and tempera on black paper (Photograph by Fred Padgelek at the home of William Rawlings, Sandersville, Georgia).

Color Plate 8. Marker and tempera on paper, 18" x 24", ca. 1982-1986 (Photograph by Andy Nasisse).

Color Plate 9. Marker, tempera, and oil pastel on blue paper, ca. 1986-1987 (Photograph by Fred Padgelek at the home of William Rawlings, Sandersville, Georgia).

Color Plate 10. Marker, crayon, and tempera on paper, 12" x 24", ca. 1985-1987 (Photograph by Andy Nasisse).

Color Plate 11. Marker, watercolor, and tempera on paper, 22" x 24", ca. 1986 (Photograph by Fred Padgelek from the collection of Fred and Mary Padgelek).

Color Plate 12. Marker, watercolor, and tempera on yellow paper, 11" x 17", ca. 1982-1986 (Photograph by Judith McWillie).

fruits of the Spirit as explained in the Bible.[49] No matter how impressive the ecstatic signs of a person, the fruit in one's life indicates whether the core of the experience is of God, of human origins, or from satanic powers.[50] Various scholars in psychology have also supported the idea of looking at the life results of a person's experience or belief system to determine the innate healthiness or unhealthiness within one's daily life and relationships.[51]

Murray the Evangelist

Unlike the majority of Southern visionary self-taught artists, it is not apparent by the art itself that Murray's subject is Christianity. One could question whether Murray is as "successful" as an evangelist as other artists whose viewers can understand the Christian meaning by looking at and reading their art. Is Murray successful as an evangelist now that he is gone and cannot talk to people about the meaning of his art and let them witness his prayer-like ritual?

The answers to these questions are clear within the precepts of Murray's faith: Murray was and is successful in his evangelical purposes because within the understanding of his faith, one is as successful as is possible if one obeys God and follows God's calling. There is nothing more to add. It is God's responsibility to use the gifts of an individual believer as God chooses. Success in evangelical terms is not determined by how many converts result from obedience to

---

[49]Ezekiel 13:3-7 provides a good example of admonishment against and warning about false prophets. Matthew 7:15-20 is a New Testament example of warning about false prophets.

[50]Galatians 5:22 lists those fruits that a believer should increasingly exhibit: "But the fruit of the spirit is love, joy, peace, patience, kindness, goodness, faithfulness, gentleness, and self-control."

[51]In regard to the benefit or harm of a religious experience and in specific reference to the biblical words, "By their fruits shall ye know them,"(Matthew 12:33), psychologist Eric Fromm writes, "If religious teachings contribute to the growth, strength, freedom, and happiness of their believers, we see the fruit of love. If they contribute to the constriction of human potentialities, to unhappiness and lack of productivity, they cannot be born of love, regardless of what the dogma intends to convey." (Eric Fromm, *Psychoanalysis and Religion* [New Haven and London: Yale University Press] 64.).

God, but by the obedience itself. Also, success in evangelical terms can have future results that are not obvious at the time. For example, in the New Testament, the Apostle Paul could not have predicted that his letters would comprise thirteen out of the twenty-seven books of the New Testament and that people would read them for (at this time) close to two thousand years and be affected in their Christian faith immeasurably. He simply did what he believed God wanted him to do. This was what Murray did also.

Murray's gift through his art centered on exhortation or praise, a gift more akin to composing poetry or music to share the spirit of one's faith rather than directly teaching or preaching. His art is a prayer language that edified Murray and others in their spiritual pilgrimmages. Within evangelical Protestantism there is the acknowledgment of different spiritual gifts. Evangelism, the gift of many visionary self-taught artists who depict the more external images of their faith and include words that often admonish people to repent and follow God, and exhortation, the gift of Murray, are two separate gifts. Evangelism focuses on the conversion of unbelievers while exhortation is often for the encouragement of believers. Although the subject of Murray's art was conversion and salvation, his method of sharing this message was not preaching, but rather presenting works of praise and demonstrations of what he believed displayed God's power.

Murray sought to create works of personal vision that extended beyond his immediate life. The spiritual themes behind his art concern the urge for deliverance, redemption, and the promise of paradise to believers. He sought to bring alive an archetypal vision and to edify a lost world. He articulated humanity's loss of spiritual community and sought an answer both in communal tenets of the past and personal poetic symbols of the present. He was molded by his faith and cultural milieu to become exhorter and evangelist in his own fashion.

4

THE LANGUAGE OF THE HOLY SPIRIT
DIRECT FROM GOD:
THE ART OF J. B. MURRAY

Murray's work reveals an underlying order that suggests a complex system of beliefs and symbols that tie his paintings and script together into an intuitive expression. At first glimpse, the modest size of his works (the largest of Murray's paintings are twenty by eighteen inches and many are considerably smaller) might not hint at the magnitude of his vision and the variety of form contained within his body of work. Yet looking closer, one discovers an instinctive richness. His work presents a vision of regeneration against the dark cataclysms of a world without God. The faith he grew up with left an indelible imprint on his mind and provided a consistent source of inspiration and imagery. His art was the journey of his call, a journey that led him by faith to experiences beyond his initial comprehension.

A Formal Description of Murray's Art

Murray did not produce his work in a linear manner; therefore, his art cannot be ordered and dated exactly. His first work can be distinguished by the materials he used, and occasionally work is seen in photographs with known dates that substantiate the time a painting was executed.[1] However, though one can recognize the first

---

[1]For example, the photograph in illustration 2 was taken by Andy Nasisse in 1982, on the day when he first met Murray; thus the work that Murray holds up in the photograph was done on or before 1982. William Rawlings talked about color plate 6b as being completed by Murray after he and Murray went to Atlanta when his work was exhibited in a group show

works by the materials used, later works cannot be put into precise chronological order. Andy Nasisse, in deliberating on the question of the chronology of Murray's work, spoke of Murray's going through phases in which he would utilize script, then perhaps later dots, and then still later grids. He would produce a number of works in a similar mode and then go on to a different style, only to later return to an earlier form of expression. Thus, one cannot assign a specific style or technique to any specific period of Murray's career.

Murray's Early Work

When Murray began to manifest his call in the form of script and painted marks in 1978, he often used surfaces that were atypical in the production of art. Though his vision was important to him and he zealously desired to share this experience through his script, drawing, and painting, he expressed his impulse on any available surface without concern for the quality of the materials. As seen in illustration 3, he even painted his script on the outside of his house. He used pencil, ball point pens, markers, and poster paint sold at the hardware store near his home to execute his early work. He created on scraps of paper, torn out pages of a Bible, adding machine tape, discarded parts of appliances, paneling, and wallboard pieces likely left over from building his simple home in 1978 (See illustrations 5-14 and color plate 1.).[2]

Color plate 1 shows Murray and a piece of paneling he painted. The faces with staring eyes are present, particularly in the middle and right section of the composition. He has put his script on the piece of paper attached at the top like a tag. In the background, more paneling

---

at the Atlanta College of Art in 1986, and Rawlings also revealed that the small bound sketchbook shown in illustrations 27 and 28, constituted the last work Murray completed before he went into the hospital and died in 1988.

[2]In Murray's southern environment, because of the isolation of many towns due to poor roads, a type of personal resourcefulness often developed that is evident in Murray's art as well as other Southern visionary self-taught artists. Stores plentiful of supplies rarely existed in small Southern towns; thus artists such as Murray turned to personal ingenuity for their creative expression.

with Murray's script can be seen. Illustrations 5-9 are examples of Murray's early script. Illustration 5 shows Murray's work created on envelopes and scrap pieces of paper. This is an example of what Murray initially brought to William Rawlings' office week after week. Illustrations 6 and 7 are examples of pages from notebooks. In illustration 7, Murray has drawn vertical columns with divisions within some of the columns, especially the first and third columns, and illustration 9, an example of Murray's script on adding machine tape, also has horizontal divisions within the script. Murray consistently uses a vertical, column-like composition throughout his career. Illustration 17 is a later example using vertical figures, and illustration 18 is a later example of the use of a column of script with horizontal sections as part of the larger composition. Illustration 11, an early work, demonstrates Murray's vertical composition he painted on a television picture tube. Illustration 20, a later example of his script, is beginning to have more of an equal emphasis on vertical and horizontal sections, similar to the grid often found in Murray's middle and later work. On the left side of illustration 13 and illustration 14 are early examples of Murray's broken mirror pattern that later became a prevalent part of many of his compositions. (See illustrations 19 and 20, and color plates 6b and 7.)

One can see rudimentary elements in Murray's earliest works that were later expressed through a larger selection of media. Impulses that developed into complex expressive color combinations exist in this beginning work and reveal themselves repeatedly throughout the years. Murray's natural talent for using color is later augmented by his use of a larger variety of paints with different properties and his practice of combining media using layers of watercolor, tempera, opaque markers, and paint sticks. As Murray initially expressed his vision to his family, members of his community and Rawlings, the marks on discarded materials demonstrated the seminal impulses of his spiritual psyche.

Murray's Middle Works

The work Murray completed after Rawlings introduced him to more conventional paint surfaces, i.e. poster board and a wider variety of markers, reaches a peak in his use of detail (See illustrations 15 and 16 and color plates 2 and 3.). The most significant difference from the early to the middle work is the methodical care Murray took in executing the latter.

In illustrations 15 and 16, Murray has included figures with details such as hair, beards, different colors, and sections of clothing. These figures also have noses, and in addition to eyes, some have mouths. In illustration 15 there are three tree shapes from the left side of the work to the middle, and there is also a tree with branches on the right side with people standing underneath. People are standing underneath the other trees, too. In illustration 15, one figure is holding out its arms and its hands include fingers. In illustration 16 there are also people with eyes, noses, mouths, and beards. The clothing is even more defined by different colors and sections. Murray has included buttons on some of the shirts. The people stand closely together as in a group of onlookers. Color plate 2 has a similar composition with vertical sections with figures that include facial details, and Murray has included some smaller figures that might represent children. Color plate 3 includes the vertical sections at the top like these other compositions, but at the bottom, figures converge or move away from a figure on the left side of the composition. Again, these figures have facial details. The figure that is vertical on the bottom of the composition has a branch-like form going off to the left, echoing the tree-like forms of illustration 15. Murray uses a composition where figures spiral away from or towards a single figure in some of his later work. (See color plates 5 and 11.)

An overall uniformity characterizes Murray's entire picture surface in these four middle pieces. In all four, he has built up the composition by intricate lines that fill every available space. The lighter value of the poster board also shows through the thin marker lines giving a unity to the works as this neutral gray color casts its tint under all of Murray's marks.

These works represent the pinnacle of Murray's concentration and time on individual pieces. After Rawlings became excited about these works of Murray's on poster board and showed them to Nasisse, Murray's individual paintings were not as detailed. He would use many dots and dashes and embellishments, but he never again included the facial details and details on the clothing of figures to the extent of these works. Towards the end of his painting, which was also the end of his life, his figures became more minimal (See illustration 17 as compared to illustrations 15 and 16 and color plates 2 and 3.).

Murray's Later Works

Murray's use of expressive lines, marks, and brush strokes, his use of mixed media seen in most of his paintings with more than one color, and his common use of many pure colors are increasingly perceptible in his later work. When one compares the early script and the early painting with his later work (illustrations 17-30 and color plates 4-12), one notices the same embellishment with dots, scribbled lines, dashes and daubs of color; yet the later example appears different because the oil pastel and the type of paper Murray used make the work look brighter. Now the work possesses an enticing depth due to Murray's aptitude in using the new materials.

Color plates 5-7 are good examples of Murray's use of oil pastel to embellish his figurative shapes with heightened color. The eyes Murray has in all his figures are more prominent as they are added with white tempera paint that contrasts to the darker values in the rest of the composition. Color plate 7 is also a good example of a new brightness created by pastels and opaque paint. As Murray added marks and accents of color in illustration 18, the tadpole-like figures on the right half of the composition are painted in a fluorescent yellow that makes them appear to float above the picture surface. Color plate 6a is an example where Murray's script stands out more than in some earlier work because of being written with a metallic silver marker on red paper, and color plate 6b shines with a brilliance of gold and silver paint pens that give the composition a layered effect where some marks recede and others come forward because of their color and opacity.

Murray had also started using colored papers that, like the poster board, give an all-over uniformity to the composition as Murray allowed the paper to show throughout the painting. Illustrations 19, 22, 23, and color plate 10 demonstrate similar compositions to earlier works such as color plates 1 and 2, but Murray's use of better quality paint in the later examples produce a richer color effect. Even with a wide choice of art materials available to him, Murray still created limited color compositions (See illustration 21.) and continued to produce pages of pure script (See illustrations 20 and 24.) throughout his ten year career.

The Structure of Murray's Art

Murray's art, although expressive and full of dynamism, demonstrates a control underlying his seemingly spontaneous compositions. As portentous guardian figures line up across a page (See illustrations 17 and 18 and color plate 4.) and other figures rush into an axis (See illustration 19 and color plate 5.), one notices an order to a composition that strangely resembles an alien world. It is not a world of chaos. The majority of Murray's art is comprised of sections of varying sizes and shapes that organize the composition into areas that fit together. A grid made up of relatively even rectangles, first seen in his early works (See illustrations 7 and 9.), is a structure Murray included in a number of later works. (See illustrations 20, 22, and 23 and color plate 6a.) He also created a structure that looks like a broken mirror or puzzle pieces that fit together. Illustrations 13 and 14 are examples of this structure in his earliest work while illustrations 19 and 20 and color plates 5, 6b, and 7 show this structure in his later works.

Murray's Script

Murray's script was the first work he produced after his first vision. Some of the script is orderly and linear (See illustrations 7-9, 18, 20, and 21.) and other script runs together forming a haphazard web of lines (See illustrations 3 and 24.[3] Some of his script is large and sprawling (See illustrations 3, 6, and the left side of 13, 24, and color plate 1.), while other script is minute and tightly controlled. (See illustrations 2, 7-9, the right side of 13, the left side of 18, 20, 21, 25-28, 30, and color plates 6a and 6b.) Within one piece the script can vary from a heightened control to a more erratic expression, such as seen in illustrations 13 and 18.

The fact that the script comprised the first expression of Murray's vision, that he consistently drew pages of pure script periodically throughout the ten years, and that it constitutes the dominant element in the last page he wrote (See illustrations 27 and 28.) indicates its importance. The script was "the language of the Holy Spirit direct from God," and always remained a part of his work, regardless of his changes in circumstances and opportunities.

Murray's Figures

Murray's figures, replete with variety, are compelling images within his art. Some works have a peering figure who peeks out from behind larger forms. For example, color plate 8 has a faded red figure on the side of the large figure that "peers" around. Other works have more developed figures with eyes, a nose, hair, and often a beard. These figures, as illustrations 15 and 16 and color plates 2 and 3

---

[3]Dr. Theodore Lewis, professor of religion with expertise in Old Testament history, Dr. Allen Godlass, professor of religion with expertise in Islamic studies, and Jared Cline, professor of linguistics, all from the University of Georgia, each looked at samples of Murray's writing to come to these conclusions. Cline also added that Murray's writing resembled Armenian and Arabic script and did not resemble Greek or Roman writing. Theodore Lewis, interview with author, transcript, Athens GA, 16 March 1993. Allen Godlass, interview with author, transcript, Athens GA, 16 March 1993. Jared Cline, interview with author, transcript, Athens GA, 15 March 1993.

demonstrate, usually have long vertical bodies with horizontal bands of color, perhaps representing clothing. Many figures do not have arms, such as Murray's vertical figures that look like pillars with rigid bodies (See color plate 4.) Murray often included developed figures who have arms, often short ones, raised up. This figure is common in the majority of Murray's works on poster board in his middle work (See illustrations 15 and 16 and color plates 2 and 3.) In illustration 2, on the left side of Murray's drawing, this figure with arms upraised includes not only features, hair, and clothing, typical of his detailed figures, but also robed arms extending to the rest of the composition or to the viewer. Color plate 8 is also an example of this figure. Murray often created fetus-shaped beings with dot eyes. Illustrations 18, 25, 26, and color plate 9 include examples of these figures. These beings' eyes consist of two dots that are the only indication that this form represents something living. In illustrations 25, 26, and color plate 9, for example, the environment swarms with these fetus shapes that give an impression of brimming life forms packed firmly against each other. All three of these compositions contain large areas of such forms with eyes that seem to stare. In illustration 25, a vertical column of script parts a sea of fetus-beings. Illustration 26, painted in a looser fashion, includes similar beings suspended in a jelly-like mass where they twist and squirm in their confinement. Illustration 18 displays these fetus shapes clearly as yellow forms standing in horizontal formation.

Murray's figures haunt his art like processional specters staring out with pleading and concern. The figures first appear in Murray's painting on scrap pieces of wood (See illustration 14 and color plate 1.) and constitute a consistent and frequent part of Murray's art throughout his ten years of art production.

Murray's Best Work

There are a variety of opinions concerning what work of Murray's represents the pinnacle of his career. Judith McWillie believes the work where Murray was in transition from pure script on scrap envelopes to figurative work with both script and figures is his most important work because in this work we witness his change from one form or understanding into something new.[4] Illustration 21 is a good example of such a work. Andy Nasisse spoke of the work Murray did on poster board after Rawlings gave Murray access to better materials, yet before the world of art discovered Murray, as some of his best work. About this work, seen in illustrations 15 and 16, and color plates 2 and 3, Nasisse stated: "Some of the early paintings and marker drawings had everything. They had the figurative elements, they had the grid, it was all there."[5] Murray spent more time on these works than he later did as he worked with increasing compulsion to do many compositions as collectors came to visit him and as he knew his time was running out when his prostate cancer began to bother him in 1987. Concerning the influence of visiting collectors, McWillie noted that Murray's amount of work changed but not the reason behind the work or its spiritual content.[6] William Arnett, a prominent Atlanta collector whose collection was the exhibit *Souls Grown Deep* in Atlanta in 1996, prefers Murray's first work done on old appliances, envelopes, and scraps around his yard because this work displays Murray's first creative impulses after his vision. (See illustrations 10, 11. 13, and color plate 1.)[7] Another view points to the work such as those shown in color plates 5, 6b, and 7 as Murray at the height of his abilities. These works demonstrate a height of Murray's complexity of form, and his use of materials to activate the surface with points of color.

Critical Response to Murray's Work

Art critics have approached Murray and his art from three distinct points of view. He has been described as an Afro-Atlantic, an Outsider, and an American Self-taught (Folk) artist. The fact that

---

[4]Judith McWillie, interview with author, transcript, Athens GA, 31 January 2000.
[5]Andy Nasisse, interview with author, tape recording, Athens GA, 18 January 1995.
[6]Judith McWillie, interview with author, transcript, Athens GA, 4 April 1994.
[7]William Arnett, conversation with author, 10 June 1995.

Murray has been defined in these various distinct ways indicates the enigmatic nature of his art and his complexity as an artist. Former gallery owner Rick Berman who represented Murray in his gallery for over a decade (approximately from 1987 to 1997), said of Murray: "He is important in that he bridges the gap between several categories. He's not really a folk artist, and he's not really an outsider artist."[8]

Murray as an Afro-Atlantic Artist

When Murray is viewed primarily as a part of the Afro-Atlantic tradition, this category emphasizes the influence of an African spirituality upon the form of his art and explains why such influence affected the area of the South where he grew up. The Afro-Atlantic designation was created by anthropologists and focuses on community and cultural continuity. When Murray and his work are seen within this classification, the focus is primarily on the form and physical attributes of his work rather than his motivation. With an emphasis on values firmly rooted in religion and spirituality, the Afro-Atlantic category centers on similarities between West African spiritual rituals and Murray's incantatory approach.

Those who have written about Murray as an Afro-Atlantic artist or as displaying African aspects in his ritual or art include Reginia Perry, Robert Farris Thompson, John Mason, Grey Gundaker, Judith McWillie, Maude Wahlman, and Andy Nasisse. John Mason described Murray's painted television picture tubes (See illustration 11.) with its "ghost reception, hence no tuning or channel changing knobs," as an "ideal appliance for modern *awo*."[9] Thompson, in referring to Murray's paintings on televisions and television picture tubes stated how Murray painted "moral messages across a television

[8]Rick Berman, interview with author, transcript, Atlanta GA, 20 May 1994.
[9]John Mason, "Old Africa, New," in *Another Face of the Diamond: Pathways Through the Black Atlantic South* (Atlanta GA: New Visions Gallery of Contemporary Art; New York: Intar Latin American Gallery, 1989), 19. An *awo* is, in West African understanding, one versed in mystery, and modern *awo* concerns the transmission of spiritual messages.

tube" and "sent them mystically, racing through time and space" as very similar to the spirit writing of the African Solomon Lumuka Kunda of Matadi, who lives among the Bakongo of Bas-Zaire.[10]

Gundaker connects Murray's script to African-Islamic protective writing and describes his script as having "a sacred thread whose unfolding and rewinding ties up problems and holds evil in check."[11] McWillie comments that when Murray described his art as "acting religion" and began "writing in the Spirit," that he "expressed a traditional West African idiom."[12] As Wahlman views Murray's art as his hedge against evil spirits, she also adjoins him with West-African notions. Nasisse links Murray's mediumistic writings, his use of water for clairvoyance, and his belief that red is the color of God to African concepts.[13] Perry connects Murray's art to "centuries old West African practices" and asserts that Diviners in West Africa still rely heavily on the use of water during the divination process to depict the future, to heal, and to dispatch good or evil spirits."[14] She believes that had Murray been born in a West African society, that he would act as such a diviner. She concludes: "Since he could not have been familiar with any aspects of West African culture firsthand, Murray's [sic] divination technique is yet another inexplicable " 'Africanism' that has survived in the African American culture of the Deep South."[15]

---

[10]Robert Farris Thompson, "The Circle and the Branch: Renascent Kongo-American Art," in *Another Face of the Diamond*, 27.

[11]Grey Gundaker, "Double Sight," in the catalogue, *Even the Deep Things of God: A Quality of Mind in Afro-Atlantic Traditional Art* (Pittsburgh PA: Pittsburgh Center for the Arts, 1999), 7.

[12]Judith McWillie, "Introduction," in *Another Face of the Diamond*, 10.

[13]Andy Nasisse, "Aspects of Visionary Art," in the catalogue, *Baking in the Sun—Visionary Images from the South* (Lafayette: University of Southwestern Louisiana, 1987), 11.

[14]Reginia Perry, "John B. Murry," in essay from *Pictured in My Mind: Contemporary American Self-Taught Art*, from the collection of Dr. Kurt Gitter and Alice Rae Yelen, (Birmingham: Museum of Art, Birmingham, 1995), 150.

[15]Ibid.

Murray as an Outsider Artist

Murray has been classified as an outsider artist more often than any other designation. The primary exhibitions that have defined Murray as an outsider are: The Los Angeles County Museum of Arts' *Parallel Visions: Modern Artists and Outsider Art/Art Brut*, at the Alpha Cubic Gallery, Tokyo; *Portraits From the Outside: Figurative Expression in Outsider Art*; and *Baking in the Sun: Visionary Images from the South*, Louisiana. This definition within the world of art emphasizes biography and seeks emotional causes behind Murray's art and his need to create. To be dubbed an outsider marks Murray as a person whose consciousness and method of responding to reality varies from mainstream society.[16]

Simon Carr provides an example of Murray and his work viewed from the outsider definition. Carr mentions Murray specifically in his article "The Visionary Body" and notes that Murray made great claims for his work being communications from God, dictated by the Holy Spirit. Yet they could only be read by the artist or person who was spiritually pure using a jar of water as a divining tool. Carr further states,

> From this apparently ordered framework, the work of Murray drives us headlong into chaos. For if the images and writing can only be "read" by the artist, if the text remains unintelligible, the meaning trapped within the artist, then there is no meaning in any broader, communicable sense. Armed with the tools of order, art, and religion, Murray's vision takes him deeper and deeper into landscapes where those tools have no meaning. Haunting stick figures, helpless, deprived of limbs, are left only their staring eyes and the incomprehensible writing that surrounds and tantalizes them. The work finally

---

[16]Sam Farber, "Portraits from the Outside: Figurative Expression in Outsider Art," in the catalogue for the exhibit, *Portraits from the Outside: Outsider Art—Art Brut*, Parsons School of Design Gallery, New York (Groegfeax Publishing, 1990), 7.

subverts the great dream of meaning, becoming like the all
out assault on dignity.[17]

Carr fails to understand that Murray's writing does not offer an
end in itself, but acts as a device that sets up circumstances important
to the exchange between Murray and the person with whom he
interacts. His writing is a prayer language of praise and homage to
God, or a point of focus, as one uses a hymn to express devotion.

Another example of commentary on Murray's work from the
outsider perspective comes from Jean-Jacques Courtine in his essay
"Raw Bodies." Courtine writes about the figures in Murray's and other
"outsiders' " work:

Just like its proportions, the limits of the body are also
problematical: hazy, uncertain, fragile, or sometimes simply
done away with. The boundaries of the body, its function as
envelope—what psychoanalysts call the "ego-skin," the body
as containing, delimiting, protecting, individualizing the
psychic identity—are constantly endangered here. So, for
example, the bodies painted by J. B. Murry [sic] have no limits
of their own.[18]

Ken Johnson, in "Significant Others," introduces Murray with a
brief visionary biography, and then in the same paragraph that
mentions Murray, he defines outsiders as having two commonalties:
"Isolation from the sociocultural milieu within which professional
artists work (which may be due to circumstances of birth, education,
or mental illness), and an unusually strong power of imagination and
fantasy."[19] It is obvious that Johnson understands Murray's belief in
his "call" and communications from God as the product of Murray's

---

[17]Simon Carr, "Visionary Bodies," in the catalogue for *Portraits From the Outside:
Outsider Art—Art Brut*, 48.

[18]Jean-Jacques Courtine, "Raw Bodies," in the catalogue for *Portraits From the Outside:
Outsider Art —Art Brut*, 37.

[19]Ken Johnson, "Significant Others," *Art in America* (June 1993): 87.

"imagination and fantasy," not as a teaching within his evangelical faith. Murray's spiritual beliefs and ritual have also been described within the larger rubric of abnormal beliefs that in a subtle way casts a question about his sanity through words that seem only to be descriptive. Roger Cardinal's essay, "Figures and Faces in Outsider Art" from *Portraits From the Outside*, provides such an example:

> Occult powers are explicitly claimed by the black visionary artist J. B. Murry [sic], who channels divine impulses into configurations half verbal, half figural, then punctuates them with tiny phantom faces suggested by pairs of eye-dots. Murray will insist on holding a bottle of pure well-water to his eyes when he reads his images, as a way to amplify their clairvoyant meaning."[20]

One suspects that Cardinal views Murray's ceremony and assumptions about his art as delusional.

Murray as a Self-Taught or Folk Artist

Finally, Murray has often been defined as an American self-taught or folk artist. Some of the books that include Murray as a folk artist are: *American Self-Taught Paintings and Drawings by Outsider Artists* by Frank Maresca and Roger Ricco; *Passionate Visions of the American South: Self-Taught Artists from 1940 to the Present* by Alice Rae Yelen; *Museum of American Folk Art Encyclopedia of Twentieth-Century American Folk Art and Artists* by Chuck and Jan Rosenak; *Pictured in My Mind:Contemporary American Self-Taught Art* from the collection of Dr. Kurt Gitter; and Alice Rae Yelen and *Black Folk Art* by Jane Livingston. In this view Murray is seen in an American historical context that emphasizes him as an artist who expressed the experi-

---

[20]Roger Cardinal, "Figures and Faces in Outsider Art," in the catalogue for *Portraits From the Outside: Outsider Art—Art Brut*, 28.

ences of his life using available material with an innate sense of aesthetic ability.

The category of self-taught by definition illuminates the fact that a substantial number of artists possess a highly developed aesthetic sensibility regardless of a lack of art training. They do not depend on encouragement or being born into a family that nurtured creativity or valued cultural awareness. These artists arise from a wide range of circumstances in society and have experienced an assortment of obstacles or advantages. Their art addresses the creative impulse and its strength of endurance that seems unaffected by hindrances to its assertion and development. With the exception of the book *Passionate Visions of the American South: Self-Taught Artists from 1940 to the Present*, by Alice Rae Yelen, the books that define Murray as a folk artist do not make much mention of his visionary experience. Yelen's book does an excellent job of presenting Murray's visionary inspiration as he is mentioned in her chapter, "Religious and Visionary Imagery."

Other Artists Who Can Be Compared to Murray

Murray's explanations of hell and the entrapment of souls beyond this world are similar to other artists who surfaced predominantly in small towns of the rural South. Sister Gertrude Morgan, (1900-1980), Howard Finster, (1915-), and James Hampton (1909-1964) are three examples of artists who each began their work after having a vision, were continually guided by visions, and saw the objective behind their art as sharing their evangelical Christian faith as did Murray. All three artists had roots in the rural South, as did Murray. The primary difference in Murray's work and almost all visionary self-taught artists is the abstraction of his work. Morgan and Finster depicted the symbols and stories of their faith in recognizable forms, such as angels, church members, and portrayals of Jesus. This is the usual approach of other visionary self-taught artists expressing their ideas from the impetus of their evangelical faith. Finster and Morgan saw themselves as preachers. Hampton saw himself as a preacher who was waiting until he finished his monumental art work to begin to teach and preach, using his art to explain the second coming of Christ. He called himself "Saint James."[21] Howard Finster calls himself "A Man of Visions" and delivers sermon-like speeches as people visit him to see his art. Sister Gertrude Morgan also considered herself a preacher and recorded her initial vision in which she believed God called her to preach through her art.[22] This is different from Murray who believed God called him to move his hand and follow his call to an undefined end. Murray did not consider himself to be a preacher, although he believed he was called to do a work for God.

Similar to Murray's script, James Hampton wrote down cryptic messages he believed he received from Jesus in small notebooks he entitled "Saint James Revelation"and believed that Jesus talked to him every night giving him instructions for his art.[23] Hampton created one monumental work of art that he worked on for over twenty years until his death. He called this work, *The Throne of the Third Heaven of the Nations Millennium General Assembly.*

Formally, one could compare Murray's work to Jackson Pollock's and Cy Twombly's, yet there is little similarity beyond outward appearances. All three created from an inner directedness and subconscious impulses, but the objectives and motivations behind the art are vastly different. Often artists like Murray whose work does resemble artists' work from the mainstream are compared as a way of lending credibility to the art of the self-taught. Yet the formal quality of Murray's work is able to speak for itself without such comparison.

---

[21]James L. Foy and James P. McMurrer, "James Hampton, Artist and Visionary," *Transcultural Aspects of Psychiatric Art*, vol. 4 of Psychiatry and Art series, Irene Jakab, ed. (Karger and Bisel, 1975), 720.

[22]Alice Rae Yelen, *Passionate Visions of the American South* (New Orleans: New Orleans Museum of Art, 1993), 321.

[23]Foy and McMurrer, "James Hampton, Artist and Visionary," 720.

Evangelical Christianity and the Art of J. B. Murray

Murray's art must be understood within a number of concepts derived from his appropriation of evangelical Christianity. Among these are the idea of "the call," conversion, evangelism, the authority of the Word, and the Holy Spirit.

The Call

Murray's belief in being "called" constituted the primary impetus for his art production. Evangelical Christians believe that all Christians receive a call from God to function as witnesses to the faith in this world by whatever means God ordains. All share God's Spirit with others; this sharing does not have to involve words. Little differentiation exists between secular and religious work because any work is spiritual if one believes that God has directed the task. One discovers this call through the guidance of the Holy Spirit who applies the precepts of the Bible to lead the individual. Murray's concept of being "called" conforms to a biblical perception he developed through the sermons in his church and his own personal response to the faith.

The core teachings of evangelicalism influenced Murray's beliefs and the formation of his art. For instance, evangelicalism's emphasis on believers sharing their faith to bring about the conversion of unbelievers is very much the purpose of Murray's art. Second, a belief in the authority of the Bible as the foundation of faith relates to the value Murray placed upon his script as he associated it with the "Word" of God. Last, the conviction that the Holy Spirit dwells within believers, giving them power to live the Christian life and speak with the wisdom of God corresponds to Murray's development of a ritual for speaking to the people who visited him.

The Conversion of Unbelievers

Murray sought to lead the viewers of his work generally from a godless life and specifically toward faith in Christ through the depiction of his "lost" figures. Such Christian conversion causes a reorientation of a person's life as one turns away from pursuing temporal interests. As an evangelical Christian, one engages in a deeper union with Christ, adheres to a moral purity, and becomes an emissary used for the spiritual welfare of other people. A righteous life is accomplished through incorporating the teachings and principles of the Bible. The conversion experience involves a transformation within an individual. Conversion is not as momentous among communicants who grow up in an area where all embrace the same faith. Historically it was important in localities like the American frontier where a new doctrine was presented and conversion repre- sented a sign of becoming initiated by God into the faith.[24] Conver- sion remains a primary concept of Southern revivalism and an initiation that sets evangelical Protestantism off as a separate fellowship.[25] The converted view life from a distinct perspective and have different values from those not converted. Corporeal abundance, intellectual achievement, and secular status are not wrong or undesirable, but these things constitute less meaningful values than redemption, spiritual evolution, wisdom from God, and the exchange of this awareness with others.[26] Evangelical Protestants accept that ordinary people can comprehend God in an intimate, powerful fashion through conversion. The fact that Murray described his figures as "the people who don't respect God" indicated his concern that those he spoke to would accept God and thus receive salvation.

Evangelism and Murray's Figures

As Murray chanted the words, "[t]he downward road is crowded. It leads about to Hell. I have always been scared of fire. It'll lead you from God. If you ain't got the Holy Spirit with you, your soul will sure

---

[24]Donald G. Matthews, *Religion in the Old South* (Chicago and London: The University of Chicago Press, 1977), 12.

[25]Ibid., 13.

[26]John B. Boles, "Conversion," *Encyclopedia of Religion in the South*, Samuel S. Hill, ed. (Macon GA: Mercer University Press, 1984), 184.

be lost. I'm scared of Hell fire. I'm scared of Hell fire. That's the reason I seek salvation from the Lord."[27] His evangelical themes about heaven and hell admonished people about the hazards of a godless existence. His work does not consist of blithe, swimming forms but seemingly of beings entangled in the mesh of their own poor choices, resulting in suffering for eternity. In illustration 19 and color plate 5, the swirling figures that scream and whose rigid bodies toss and bounce around as if in a world without gravity are Murray's people who live without God. The very nature of the staring eyes and bodies stiff with fear indicate their peril. The limbless state of the figures further emphasizes Murray's concept that these living forms float, powerlessly suspended in a spiritual limbo. Their demise registers surprise, judging from the stark stares and, on some beings, screaming mouths. They radiate from a center into confusion and darkness, which constitutes a biblical description of the situation "evil people" can expect.[28] Concerning the figures in his work, Murray stated, "[God] show me evil folks. . . . That's why all these different pictures, all the pictures done before the evil folks on judgment day. . . . Evil folks, bad folks, mean folks don't serve God and they come against God. And the dry tongue they can say 'Amen' but they don't mean it from the heart."[29]

Murray's disembodied beings who looked like squirming amoebas crammed into an area too small for them to maneuver relate to his words: "The downward road is crowded. These signs is the signs of the downward road. It's crowded with unbelieving souls."[30] These words relate to the biblical admonishment concerning the "narrow gate" that leads to salvation[31] and that also advocate that the path to God is much less populated than the downward path that leads to self-

---

[27]Transcript (in author's possession) of J. B. Murray, interview with Judith McWillie, video recording, Mitchell GA, 31 May 1986. These words were sung by Murray.
[28]Matthew 8:12, 13:42, 22:13, 24: 51, 25:30, and Luke 13:28.
[29]Murray, transcript of videotaped interview.
[30]Ibid.
[31]Matthew 7:13-14.

destruction.[32] Illustrations 25 and 26 display thick masses of the overpopulated godless beings contained and trapped within a circumscribed area. In illustration 25 a band of script splits an area of helpless-looking living forms that are tightly packed together. In illustration 26 a block of script at the bottom of a column and rectangular sections of script at the top pronounce Murray's message to the wriggling forms suspended in a red environment. The living forms look imprisoned and powerless because they have no bodies or arms and are unable to move in the cramped space. In illustrations 22 and 23 and color plate 10, Murray painted entire compositions where bodiless heads stare out helplessly.

Works similar to those in illustrations 25 and 26 Murray himself described as depicting lost souls trapped in a state between life on earth and their ultimate eternal destination:

> This one, this is the evil people. They're blocked, they can't get out. That's what is happening at the top. They can't get out. . . . The top part suppose to be the earth and they can't get out. That's a restless place, till judgment day come. Living in a restless place and they can't get out. The world's still haunting them where they at. That's when you can't rest. They restless for what they wanna do and they can't get out.[33]

Murray's words suggest that he believed in a waiting place where souls go after physical death which exists between the physical world and heaven and hell. Not an idea sustained by evangelical Protestantism, this concept may have West African spiritual roots associated with the belief that there exists a spiritual domain of ancestors who interact with people living on earth, yet are spirits. Within evangelical Protestantism, an idea close to this understanding involves the realm of angels and demons who interact with the living. The confining

---

[32]"Downward road" refers to people who take the wider road of worldliness that leads to spiritual poverty and destruction, according to Murray. Murray, transcript of videotaped interview.

[33]Ibid.

nature of the area of the beings in illustrations 25 and 26 visually indicates the idea of entanglement within a sphere that exists between the world we know and the next.

Murray depicted representations of heaven and earth in compositions divided either horizontally or vertically. Murray explained to Rawlings that the figures on the bottom of color plate 9 consisted of people on earth of distinct races, sex and circumstances, indicated by Murray's painting the figures in a variety of colors.[34] Murray explained to Rawlings that the top part of the image depicts people in heaven where all look the same because they have heavenly bodies not distinguishable externally. In the top part of the painting, the beings in heaven are not confined, but swim freely and drift through their environment with ease. On the bottom part of the painting the black lines that outline the figures act as ropes which tie them together. Not only are these bottom shapes of different colors, but they are not as mobile. Murray depicts the binding nature of external appearance on earth as opposed to the freedom of eternal souls clothed in their heavenly bodies. Murray's figures that peer around the sides of larger beings suggest the evangelical Christian idea of protection (See color plate 8.) As Murray expressed it, "You have to pull close to God for God to stand between us and make a footstool out of our enemies. . . . I've got a few enemies around now. They still work at me, and the Lord speaks to that. I have to hold on to His unchanging hand, and that's what I'm going to do."[35] Color plate 8, where a large figure stands stalwartly in the midst of what looks like a vast conflagration, with several individuals clinging to and peering around its sides, visually relates to God protecting believers from the inferno of hell. The staring eyes and the clinging nature of the three small figures that stand close to the large figure indicate that these beings use the large form for protection.

---

[34]William Rawlings, interview with author, tape recording, Sandersville GA, 3 June 1993.
[35]Murray, transcript of video taped interview.

The idea of protection relates to the tenet of evangelism that one of the primary reasons a person converts to Christianity is to secure God's protection both in this world and the world to come. Protection in this world does not suggest an easier life for the believer but rather that suffering has a purpose: "And we know that in all things God works for the good of those who love Him, who have been called according to His purpose."[36]

In keeping with the teachings of evangelical Christianity that encourage caring for the spiritual and physical well-being of oneself and others, Murray possibly used certain works as a personal supplication for spiritual and physical healing. In relation to his own healing, the scrotum-like shape in illustration 21 could represent a prayer for his prostate cancer. This work incorporates red lines that look like blood vessels and living tissue. The composition, filled with writing that surrounds the living tissue, possibly acted as words of prayer that include a request for healing. During one of Nassise's visits with Murray, Murray's foot was sore and hurting him. Murray put a piece of paper on the floor and traced around the aching foot, seeming to associate drawing around his foot with healing it. It is not known whether Murray later made this foot tracing into a painting with writing around it in a similar way to illustration 21.[37]

The red lines in Murray's work (See illustrations 12-14 and color plates 1 and 6b.) relate to another explanation he gave for his symbolism. Concerning the eternal demise of the ungodly that Murray depicted, he expressly spoke of his red lines: "The red is torment and those lines lead into torment and there is no way out. It's up and down in torment. Torment is a dead end for the souls."[38] Illustration 14 provides an example of an early work where heads with either no bodies or undeveloped tadpole-like torsos float in an environment of red lines that knot and bind the pieces of the painting together. As

[36]Romans 8:28.
[37]Andy Nasisse, interview with author, tape recording, Athens GA, 22 April 1997.
[38]Murray, transcript of videotaped interview.

beings are enmeshed in red cords that tie the separate forms together, Murray's work again issues a warning of the consequences of sin.

Illustrations 7, 9, 13, 20, and 21 incorporate red lines within Murray's script. This inclusion accents the same admonishment. In illustration 20, red lines, broken and jagged, permeate the entire composition. A continuous red line encompasses the script on the page, circumscribing the area of writing. Murray's lines of torment contain the message of the script, similar to how blocks of writing define the cramped space of the amoebae-like beings in illustrations 25 and 26 that connect to Murray's message of souls caught in a holding space between this life and their eternal destination.

Dots, dashes, and daubs of pigment embellish various figures in Murray's later pieces. (See color plates 5 and 7.) When Murray was asked to explain daubs that resembled pink beads (See color plate 7.), he replied that they depict ". . . evil that's in different looks and different fashions. . . . They have different uniforms from one another to be bragged on. That's what that is."[39] Murray exhorted against people's practice of emphasizing their external appearance more than the internal state of their souls. Within his faith, he knew that "man looks upon the outside condition but God looks on the heart."[40] In color plate 7, Murray's dots and daubs of pink and white, on black pastel paper indicate the decorations people use to embellish their outer appearance.

Murray believed that a war between righteousness and evil raged daily on an invisible spiritual level and some works clearly reflect this spiritual battle. (See illustration 18 and color plate 4.) Within his fundamentalist Christian view, only two varieties of spirits existed: those of God and those of Satan. All who choose not to follow Christ follow Satan, who exists as the god of the world. When Murray articulated his ideas concerning "evil people," he did not refer to people who do heinous deeds, necessarily, but those who have not

---

[39]Ibid.
[40]1 Samuel 16:7.

embraced Christ. Murray's words substantiate his belief in a spiritual battleground surrounding him:

> That is a evil picture as Satan was in Heaven. . . . I thank you Jesus for giving me this mind for drawing at your will against [Satan's] favor and his design and his meanness. He against God and the Holy Spirit. He's for gamin' and can't help. He mislead peoples and give peoples the wrong line from God. He invaded against the gates of Heaven, against God's Holy Spirit, Amen.[41]

Murray occasionally spoke in eschatological terms referencing the Book of Revelation, a book of the Bible abundant with descriptions of battles and a final war between good and evil. Again Murray's words suggest his concern for confronting the forces of evil in battle: "There are many things to be, but yet, not the end. And the first thing. . . a spiritual army. God gonna raise up on the water a nation. Rise up on the sea. And can't no man war against it. We will tear down the wall, and there is nothing man can do."[42] In some of Murray's pieces, beings appear like soldiers standing in formation. (See illustration 18 and color plate 4.) These protectors with attenuated bodies form an impenetrable rampart, impeding any force it might encounter. Such stalwart figures represent Murray's soldiers in the battle against the onslaught of the forces of darkness. In color plate 4 the figures rigidly stand together expressionlessly taking their place in the army of God. The notion of believers who have God's Spirit on guard against the forces of wickedness in the world recurs in numerous Bible verses taught within evangelical churches: "For our struggle is not against flesh and blood, but against the rulers, against the authorities, against the powers of this dark world and against the spiritual forces of evil in the heavenly realms."[43]

---

[41]Murray, transcript of videotaped interview.
[42]Ibid.
[43]Ephesians 6:12.

But the Bible also affirms that the forces of light are strong enough to subdue the evil of the world through the prayers and God-led actions of Christian believers.[44] Figures with arms raised are common throughout Murray's work and Murray was clearly familiar with raising arms in prayer: "It's a custom in the church. Lord I stretch my hands to Thee. There's no other help I know. Stretching is all the help they know."[45] These figures are praying. In illustration 16 and color plate 2 a group of tall people with detailed features and clothing stand together. Several of the figures have raised arms. In illustration 2 the figure with its arms elevated wears a robe, and in color plate 8 this type of figure is set apart and distinguished by its size and the intensity of its facial expression and coloration. In both of these latter illustrations Murray invested this figure with an extraordinary command. Perhaps his emphasis demonstrates the power of prayer, a pivotal teaching within evangelicalism.

The Authority of the Word

The second foundational belief of evangelical Christianity that profoundly affected Murray concerns the authority of the Bible, the Word of God. A familiar verse supporting the inspiration of the Bible is from 2 Peter: "Above all, you must understand that no prophecy of Scripture came about by the prophet's own interpretation. For prophecy never had its origin in the will of man, but men spoke from God as they were carried along by the Holy Spirit."[46] Within evangelicalism the word of God stands apart and is invested with an authority that keeps the beliefs of the faith from veering from a biblical foundation. Most evangelicals believe God inspired the words of the Bible. At one extreme, the belief of biblical inerrancy holds that the Bible constitutes the literal record of God's words spoken to the biblical authors. This perception of the Bible establishes the heart of

---

[44]1 John 2:15-17.
[45]Murray, transcript of videotaped interview.
[46]2 Peter 1: 20.

fundamentalism. Proponents of inspiration support this belief with scripture itself. Second Timothy 3:16 provides an example of this: "All Scripture is God-breathed and is useful for teaching, rebuking, correcting and training in righteousness. . . . " Critics of this assertion say the Bible did not originally support the concept of biblical inerrancy, but the idea came about through verses added in subsequent interpretations.[47] A point of view that represents the liberal extreme of evangelical Protestantism supports the belief that the Bible contains the word of God, although various interpretations altered the text through time. Generally, however, evangelical congregations acknowledge the authority of the Bible, a characteristic that distinguishes them from denominations that are not evangelical. Evangelicals define "authority" as the power to command, a term that designates how one understands scripture and how closely one adheres to the tenets as a rule and ordering device in one's life.[48]

The Authority of the Word and Murray's Script

When Murray's hand formed the sometimes uniform, and at other times erratic, hurried rows of his script, he did not offer arbitrary marks but what he believed constituted words that enlightened his audience about faith in God and humanity's accountability, which is what evangelicals believe God's word offers. Murray used his script to give supremacy to the words he spoke to people. When Murray declared, "Your Word, Your Name, Your Power,"[49] he confirmed that his veneration for God's word offered a commanding force that impelled him to generate volumes of script as an admonition for all to whom he handed his inspired writing. Murray's belief in the power of the Word of God gave his script command by association, and such a belief compelled him enthusiastically to share this word with

---

[47]Thomas W. Mann, "Authority of the Bible," *Encyclopedia of Religion in the South,* Samuel S. Hill, ed. (Macon GA: Mercer University Press, 1984), 96.
[48]Ibid., 95-96.
[49]Murray, transcript of videotaped interview.

everyone God brought to him. Murray further expressed the reverence he had for the Word of God:

> I will stand on His Word even if the preachers don't. There is nothing He starts but what he don't finish it. . . . Like death comes in the twinkling of an eye, his Word and what he tells you comes in the twinkling of an eye. And every knee will bow. If you don't have that knee of faith you are still a long way from God. It's His will that we do everything that His law requires us to do.[50]

Various examples of Murray's script resemble the appearance of pages in some Bibles. For instance, chapters in the Bible will often begin with a large capital letter encased in an elaborately designed rectangle, set apart from the rest of the page by its distinct ornamentation. The dense rectangular form at the top of illustration 8 reflects Murray's approximation of such pages with the dark irregular shape drawn with dense black lines representing a beginning capital letter. This composition also has similarities to illuminated manuscripts or pages from the Bible that include illustrations of the text. Another association with the visual appearance of the Bible are Murray's books (See illustrations 27 and 28.) and his pages of pure script. (See illustrations 6-9, 20, and 24.) The fact that some of Murray's script is intricately minute (See illustrations 7-9.) echoes the tiny print of many Bibles. Some of the script in vertical columns has similarities to the design of a page of the Bible which is often divided into columns of words. (See illustration 7.) Also, in connection to a biblical page, Murray's underlining in red in illustrations 7 and 9, in addition to his description of the red lines that lead to torment, correspond to the red print of the New Testament that identifies the words of Jesus.

Murray indicated by the materials he used, the format he chose, and the prominence of the script in his work, that there existed a sacredness within the writing he executed. He often included script

---

[50]Ibid.

isolated in a contrasting material (i.e. metallic silver and gold markers) on a sheet of paper, giving it a place of reverence, with a tablet-like presentation. (See illustration 29 and color plate 6a.) This place of privilege and setting the script apart by way of contrasting media suggests the conception of the stone tablets on which Moses received the Ten Commandments directly from God. For example, the script of color plate 6a looks like gilded monoliths since four rectangles of silver grace the middle of the composition and compose the primary focal point. Murray's script on adding machine tape (See illustration 9.), has a scroll-like appearance, a format comparable to ancient biblical documents written on parchment.[51] This example is separated into sections of script either by color or by lines. Murray's custom of presenting rolled-up bundles of script tied with string to William Rawlings also is reminiscent of ancient sacred texts of the biblical scribes being presented in ceremony.

Crosses that include script commonly appear in Murray's works dated after 1982. Sometimes Murray's crosses are evenly distributed in a work while other times he seemed to place them randomly throughout areas of script. Murray often drew crosses at the beginning of the first line of script and sometimes at the top and bottom of pages as in a dedication or conclusion to a message. Murray also included crosses on a line of script he added to the back of his drawing paper. (See illustration 30.) Nasisse believes this line of script is Murray's signature. In Murray's last book (See illustrations 27 and 28.) each page includes crosses, which is typical in the sketchbook as a whole.

The Ministry of the Holy Spirit

Evangelicals believe that the Holy Spirit dwells within and empowers believers to perform God's will and achieve the internal satisfaction of a life lived with a vital spiritual connection. Murray believed that the Holy Spirit gave him the words of his script and influenced the words he spoke to people as he asked for a "louder

---

[51]Murray likely heard of ancient biblical scrolls in his church.

word up." The power of the indwelling Holy Spirit pledged to believers offers a third distinguishing tenet of evangelical Christianity that makes this faith a powerful force for transformation and productiveness in a believer's life. Evangelicals believe that the indwelling Holy Spirit performs as a counselor and guide. Some of the ways a believer receives such guidance is through personal prayer and the prayers of others, the words of the Bible, and the words of other people. Some of the more ecstatic manifestations of the Holy Spirit are healing, prophecy and glossolalia (speaking in tongues).[52] Murray's spirit script compares to glossolalia in that both practices involve an esoteric language believed to be produced by the Spirit of God. The majority of evangelical Protestant churches do not encourage the more ecstatic gifts publicly, although members might exercise these gifts privately or in small groups. Because the New Testament refers to these gifts, evangelicals do not disavow their existence, although debate exists about whether certain gifts disappeared or continued after biblical times. Before 1960 such phenomena as healing and glossolalia were principally found in churches with poor, uneducated congregations. After 1960, however, the spiritual gifts of healing and especially glossolalia began penetrating most mainline denominations, including the Roman Catholic Church. This movement was initially termed "Neopentecostalism" because it had some similarities to Pentecostalism.[53]

The Holy Spirit and Murray's Ritual

As previously established, Murray maintained that the guidance of the Holy Spirit was responsible for his ministry and his art. Murray

---

[52]Watson E. Mills, "Glossolalia,"*Encyclopedia of Religion in the South*, Samuel S. Hill, ed. (Macon GA: Mercer University Press, 1984), 305. The common definition of glossolalia is utterance of incomprehensible and seemingly random vocal sounds. The sounds seem effortless and the structure of the sounds is complex. It has been described as sounding like a chant or calypso.

[53]John Wilson, "Charismatic Movements," *Encyclopedia of Religion in the South*, Samuel S. Hill, ed. (Macon GA: Mercer University Press, 1984), 144.

believed that the script, the painting, the ceremony of gazing at his work through a jar of water, and the words God wanted him to declare were all equally inspired by this Spirit who, according to the Bible, equals God Himself as the third Person of the Trinity. Murray believed the Holy Spirit led him to evolve a ritual to present to his audience. As more people visited Murray from outside his community to see his work, he addressed and communicated his message to people he did not know and who were unlike him in many ways. Although from the beginning of his art Murray used a jar of water as an interpreting device for deciphering the message of his compositions, the ritualistic aspect likely became accentuated as more people came to see him.

The ritual of the Holy Spirit guiding Murray as he looked through the jar of well water and spoke to visitors encompassed a part of his calling as important to him as his script and painting. In his words, "You see, the spoken word of God, it's different from the Spirit. . . ."[54] To Murray, the ceremony surrounding his art presented another form of the manifestation of the Holy Spirit. He believed that after his initial vision he could ask God questions and receive answers by looking through the jar of water. Murray remarked upon his use of the medium of water to pose questions: "Jesus, I thank you for the knowledge you give me to go by. You gave me the mind to ask you questions with water."[55] Concerning the use of water in Murray's ritual, Nasisse said that the water was vital to Murray who insisted that "this is the water Jesus walked on."[56] Nasisse also indicated that the water from Murray's well was a significant symbol because the well extended deeply into the ground.

To William Rawlings, Murray's ritual was the public face of his private conviction. Murray needed a way to present his work and his message. He evolved a rite, a ceremony to augment the visual vocabulary of evangelism that had asserted itself in his iconography.

---

[54]Murray, transcript of videotaped interview.
[55]Ibid.
[56]Murray, transcript of videotaped interview.

Both the art and the ritual were means to communicate the supernatural. Concerning Murray's ritual Rawlings stated:

> Some of [the ritual] was J. B. hyping the public. Some of it was J. B. the showman. The real J. B. was quite serious about it, however. Let's just pretend that you are deeply religious and enjoy praying but you don't pray in public or don't pray in the street but you pray in the privacy of your home. But if you're called upon in a public gathering to give a moving and monumental prayer, you would do so and be proud of it. So this was J. B.'s public display of his private work.[57]

Robert Farris Thompson, the author of *Flash of the Spirit, Four Moments of the Sun,* and other works on African and African-American art and symbolism, after visiting Glascock County to see Murray, wrote about the creation of Murray's work and the ritual that was a part of the sharing of his art. Thompson described Murray's state of mind during his rite as more trance-like than Rawlings observed. Thompson witnessed a scene more akin to African and Christian practices mixing in a realm of dream, memory, and spiritual connection. Thompson described Murray's ritual:

> I asked a question about his calligraphic drawings. By way of answer, he picked up white paper, took my brush-pen and let it move across the paper. A slightly wavy, sometimes broken line appeared. "I ain't moving it; it's moving itself." His eyes narrowed. His gaze became distant, dreamy. The pen nearly fell off the page. Silence. Suddenly, the [S]pirit. The single line which initiated the work was overwritten with bursts of figuration, sometimes connected and flowing, and sometimes not. The dynamics of his spirit-writing were akin to music. Density and noise. Then silence. Then dancing wire-like curlicues and gnostic "letters." Returning silence. Then

---

[57]Rawlings, interview, 3 June 1993.

miniature figurations expanding into larger sequences, like stanzas, finished and controlled. When the drawing was finished, he lifted up a glass of clear water, asking the Lord to witness this work "in His water."[58]

To Rawlings, Murray did not go into an altered state, but through his developing ritual sought to embellish his evangelical message for an audience; to Thompson, Murray's condition during his ritual had aspects of a mystical state.

Evangelical Christianity's examples and foundational tenets provided Murray with a mission that inflamed his passionate concern for the people whom he believed God wanted him to address. Like a biblical prophet with a burning aspiration, Murray produced his art. He shared the wisdom of eternal salvation in what he believed was "the language of the Holy Spirit, direct from God."

---

[58]Robert Farris Thompson, "Writings Witnessed Through the Waters," remarks included on the invitation to the Rosa Esman Gallery, New York, 29 April-17 May 1985, where Murray's work was exhibited.

5

THIS WELL IS DEEP AND NEVER GO DRY:

IMPLICATIONS OF J. B. MURRAY AND THE VISIONARY SELF-TAUGHT ARTIST

Andy Nasisse recognized the formal quality of Murray's work as soon as he was aware of it. He credits Murray's art as having an influence upon the evolution of ideas in twentieth century art because Murray's work was as good as artists accepted within the mainstream canon of art, yet he had no formal training and no concept that he was even doing art. Therefore, Murray and other self-taught artists and visionaries expanded the definition of who could be considered an artist and why. Nasisse also responded to Murray's passion and drive behind his work that influenced how the work looked. Further commenting on Murray's importance as an artist, Nasisse stated:

> Murray has many different levels of importance. In a universal sense, he is an individual who exhibits an authenticity in the work he does and is truly connected to a large energy or spirit. His importance extends into many spheres—to humanity as a whole and to the art world— because of his innocence and his connection to an important state. I don't believe that Murray was taught or learned what he did from an outside influence. He worked from the inside out.[1]

---

[1]Andy Nassise, telephone conversation with author, 5 June 1994.

Judith McWillie terms Murray's art as "extensions of his charismatic experience" and also recognizes the formal success of his work that sprung from his beliefs[2]:

> Murray is important for all artists. He was a part of a community and had a healthy reason for doing art. For giving. Murray gave his vision regardless of ostracism and misunderstanding. America had two times of covert spirituality—transcendentalism and abstract expressionism. The lives of the abstract expressionists were so tragic because of their alcoholism, isolation, loneliness and self-destruction that after that people ran from the spiritual. But Murray is just as good as Pollock but he wasn't isolated and lonely. Murray is important as an alternative example for artists. . . .[3]

One must ask what J. B. Murray and other visionary self-taught artists offer to our conception of American art and what their emergence and popularity at this time in history signifies. The acceptance of the self-taught artist is not new; there is a history in the twentieth century of an influence and appreciation of art from outside the mainstream. Because of certain characteristics of contemporary times, however, artists such as Murray can conceivably impact the world of art in a manner never before possible.[4]

The Acceptance of Self-taught Artists in the Twentieth Century

It is necessary to trace the history of the acceptance of self-taught artists in the twentieth century to understand the difference in their most recent popularity beginning in the 1980s. Before World War I, interest in art produced from divergent cultures began with a focus on

---

[2]Judith McWillie, telephone conversation with author, 28 June 1993.
[3]Ibid.
[4]There is also a history in the eighteenth and nineteenth centuries as many ordinary people decorated their houses and businesses with handcrafted figures, weather vanes, advertisements, and hand-painted signs.

tribal art by avant-garde modernists who considered it to be a formal alternative to art from the academic tradition. In America, various collectors (for instance, Dr. Albert C. Barnes) began to acquire African art along with collections of work by Cezanne, Matisse, and other modernists. The collecting of African art was furthered by the African-American scholar, Alain Locke, a philosophy professor at Howard University, who himself accrued an impressive group of works that he used to demonstrate the cultural heritage of Afri-can-Americans prior to slavery. African art also gained wide exposure and acceptance with the exhibit African Negro Art, presented at the Museum of Modern Art in New York in 1935.[5] The "discovery" and embrace of African and Oceanic art by European artists such as Matisse and Picasso was followed by the "discovery" of American folk painting and sculpture.[6] During the 1920s various exhibitions examined the form and validity of the newly discovered folk and self-taught artists. One of the most important milestones for indicat-ing a broader interest and acceptance of this work was the opening of the American Folk Art Gallery in New York City in 1931.[7]

An interest in self-taught artists surfaced again in America in the late 1960s and early 1970s. This was a period when an impulse for a more democratic culture and a rejection of established conventions promoted a desire to broaden definitions of art.[8] Contemporary artists were the first to seek out self-taught artists and focus on expressions that were outside the boundaries of the "mainstream." From a formal and expressive point of view, self-taught art meshed with the aesthetic experiments, the blurring of boundaries, and an emphasis on pluralism

---

[5]James L. Foy and James P. McMurrer, "James Hampton, Artist and Visionary," *Transcultural Aspects of Psychiatric Art*, vol. 4 of Psychiatry and Art series, Irene Jakab, ed. (New York: Karger and Bisel, 1975), 75.

[6]Daniel Robbins, "Folk Sculpture without Folk," in *The Artist Outsider: Creativity and the Boundaries of Culture*, Michael D. Hall and Eugene W. Metcalf, Jr. with Roger Cardinal, eds. (Washington and London: Smithsonian Institution Press, 1994), 46.

[7]Ibid., 44.

[8]Joanne Cubbs, "Rebels, Mystics and Outsiders," *The Artist Outsider: Creativity and the Boundaries of Culture*, Michael D. Hall and Eugene W. Metcalf, Jr. with Roger Cardinal, eds., (Washington and London: Smithsonian Institution Press, 1994), 86.

prevalent in the mid-1960s. Artists explored new materials and formats, created installations and environmental work, and were engaged in various alternative modes of expression.[9] By the early 1970s there was a renewed interest in narrative, figurative, and representational styles of art, specifically with New Image Painting and Neo-Expressionism.[10] There also was more work created that dealt with moral, political, and social issues, and the use of literature and allegory as subject-matter was now permissible and not seen as retrograde. Such a climate openly received the work of the self-taught artist and visionary, who generally produced narrative, representational, and figurative work with a social or religious content.[11] The self-taught artists fit well into the visual and philosophic tenor of these times.

In the 1980s, a difference in the type of self-taught art gradually emerged. On 6 March 1981, an important exhibition was held at the Philadelphia College of Art titled *Transmitters: The Isolate Artist in America*. This was one of the first American art exhibits in the twentieth-century in which self-taught art featured drawing, painting, and sculpture not derived from a craft or folk tradition. The majority of artists in the show worked with found objects and had an expressionistic style, comparable with the "high" art of the time.[12] Another art exhibit, *Black Folk Art in America* curated by Jane Livingston and John Beardsley, opened at the Corcoran Art Gallery in Washington DC, in 1982 and toured to Los Angeles, New York City, Detroit, Houston, Louisville, and Birmingham. Like its predecessor, this exhibit was also limited to "expressionistic" painting, drawing, and sculpture. The show featured twenty African-American artists, most of whom lived in the South.[13]

---

[9]Joseph Jacobs, *A World of Their Own: Twentieth-Century American Folk Art* (Newark: The Newark Museum, 1995), 24.

[10]Bruce D. Kurtz, *Contemporary Art 1965-1990* (Englewood Cliffs NJ: Prentice Hall, 1992), 8.

[11]Jacobs, *A World of Their Own*, 26.

[12]Ibid., 31.

[13]Ibid.

Thomas McEvilley, in his 1997 article "The Missing Tradition," suggests that the most current recognition of the self-taught artist exposes "some of the repressed material of the American visual psyche."[14] In his article, McEvilley writes about two exhibits of African-American self-taught artists, *Thornton Dial: Remembering the Road* and *Souls Grown Deep: African-American Vernacular Art of the South*, held in Atlanta as part of the Cultural Olympiad of the 1996 Olympic games. The first exhibit, at the Carlos Museum of Emory University, featured Alabama artist Thornton Dial, Sr., and displayed seventy-five of his paintings, works on paper, and sculptures. The second exhibit included over 300 pieces of art by forty artists, and was set up at City Hall East.[15] In regard to displaying the works of the African-American self-taught artists in these exhibits, McEvilley commented, "Surely the emergence of this body of work into wider consciousness is a historic element of our time. . . . This art is performing the powerful task of revealing hidden forces within the matrix of history."[16]

One must wonder what these "hidden forces" are that McEvilley contends are being overlooked in America and what caused the reception of self-taught artists at this point in history. While the aesthetic qualities of this art have been widely appreciated for many decades, the artists themselves were rarely seen as instigators of this acceptance, nor was their philosophy as artists given credence. Andy Nasisse, speaking as an artist, early collector, and appreciator of the work of self-taught visionaries, contends that one reason for the earlier neglect of self-taught artists outside of a craft tradition involves the fact that "much of their work was eccentric and did not fit within the concept of modernism. Therefore, most people overlooked them until a few artists, some of whom were themselves eccentric, began to

---

[14]Thomas McEvilley, "The Missing Tradition," *Art in America* (May 1997): 79.

[15]Ibid. The work of both exhibits was primarily from the collection of William Arnett. Murray had fifteen to twenty pieces of art in *Souls Grown Deep*, which were displayed in one room.

[16]Ibid., 137.

champion the work because they recognized it as having validity and possessing an important formal and expressive dimension."[17]

Joanne Cubbs, former curator of folk art at the High Museum of Art in Atlanta, Georgia, maintains that in the 1980s there occurred within the world of art an interrogation of the canon that was unprecedented, spurred on by the phenomenon popularly termed "multiculturalism." There involved a kind of intellectual questioning of the hierarchical elitist value system underlying the appreciation of certain kinds of art forms. She claims, "The interest in self-taught art and the world of discourse in art was in part based on the opening up of the canon."[18] Andy Nasisse adds that a disenchantment with academia and status quo, along with the social and political revolution in the sixties and the Vietnam War, indicated a cultural milieu ready to accept new definitions of art.[19]

The interrogation of ideas assumed to support a privileged structure in society that left many powerless opened up consideration of artists who were consigned to the fringes of society. Previously marginalized groups such as women, African-Americans, and gays were being included as an entity in American culture as never before.[20]

---

[17]Andy Nasisse, interview with author, tape recording, Athens GA, 22 April 1997.

[18]Joanne Cubbs, phone interview with author, taped interview, 25 April 1997. Here the "canon" refers to the historic inclusion of certain art and artists as being a part of a sacrosanct collection of masterpieces and masters. This collection is believed by many people today to be too narrow and exclusive of art and artists outside a Western European paradigm.

[19]Nasisse interview, 22 April 1997.

[20]Irving Sandler, *Art of the Postmodern Era: From the Late 1960s to the Early 1990s* (New York: Harper Collins Publisher, Inc., 1996), 341. In the 1970s, various artists and art critics sought to uncover the way language supported thinking that was linked to a Eurocentric, male- dominated power structure within capitalism. An ethnocentric mode of thinking had also been recognized as the assumption behind colonialism and, by extension, modernism. The primary goal of theorists and intellectuals at this time was "decentering" or challenging the hierarchy. They questioned the idea of a "mainstream" in modernist art and the dominance of Western culture. They challenged the idea of genius and patriarchal power. Their primary mode of challenge was through the theory of deconstruction. (337). Jacques Derrida, the French philosopher who was one of the first to compose the theory of deconstruction, declared that personal identity and the constructs of society are formed by

Another reason for the present popularity of this work involves accessibility, either actual or perceived. Collectors who could not afford to buy the work of long-established artists such as Jasper Johns or Robert Rauschenberg, for instance, could buy the work of self-taught artists. Rick Berman, a former Atlanta gallery owner who represented Murray's art along with other self-taught artists, believes that after the Corcoran Show in the early 1980s, the new collectors became interested because the opportunity arose to buy great art for very little money.[21] William Eiland, Director of the Georgia Museum of Art and collector of self-taught art, adds that "when the prices of this art rise. . . [one] will see a wane in the general interest."[22]

Also related to the accessibility of the self-taught artists, Eiland adds that these artists became recognized in recent times because of the availability of better communication and transportation: "We were able to locate them; one could drive around, find them and photograph them."[23] They also offered their acquaintance and friendship. Between 1960 and 1974, more than two hundred self-taught artists were introduced to the world of art, and this search has escalated more recently as collectors comb the backwoods and rural areas of America.[24]

One spurious assumption about the symbolic and aesthetic accessibility of these artists involves a perception of simplicity that can be associated with the art of the self-taught. Because of their depiction of familiar scenes from the Bible and everyday life, the symbolism and subject-matter of the work may at first seem easy to penetrate. This idea does not apply as much to Murray, whose work is abstract, as to self-taught artists like Sister Gertrude Morgan and Howard Finster, who use more recognizable imagery. Evangelical Protestantism, the ideology that informed the work of Murray,

---

language. The philosophy of deconstruction challenged historic modes of thinking by which the social order in Western civilization had achieved dominance (340).

[21]Rick Berman, written responses to questions from author, 10 March 1997.

[22]William Eiland, interview with author, tape recording, Athens GA, 12 June 1997.

[23]Ibid.

[24]Jacobs, A World of Their Own, 26.

Morgan, and Finster, is generally accessible because of the historical connections between this faith and American identity. Also, because evangelicalism emphasizes the conversion of unbelievers, it is a faith that is widely disseminated to the public through publishing and the media. Yet the zeal to "witness in the faith" inherent in the motives of these artists can lead one to underestimate the complexity of this work.

Joanne Cubbs, for example, is skeptical about depicting the self-taught artist as the "common man, or simple or ordinary, because often these artists are some of the most extraordinary individuals among us."[25] The art of the self-taught is often understood as having universal meanings that do not require the viewers or audience to think critically about how they experience the formal aspects of the art or its deeper relevance. This is an erroneous assumption and represents a dangerous part of the mythology of the genre. One must recognize that the work comes from a complex context.[26] This art is not simple; it is specific and contextually based. Yet the perception that "you really don't have to know much about art or even about what that art is saying to appreciate it," has in part, contributed to its economic and popular success.[27]

The work of self-taught artists is often seen as charming and entertaining rather than confrontational. The artists themselves are perceived as spontaneous, pure, and uncomplicated, with a vibrancy and sense of life that is rare and admirable. However, this kind of over-simplification can mask a tendency to make those who one perceives as different into what one needs them to be without considering the challenges they offer. For example, we can admire Murray's fervor and the zeal that produced his art, yet not take his warnings of hell and deep concern for people's salvation seriously as he did. We can dismiss the message of Murray's art because we see him as sincere, though simplistic.

---

[25]Cubbs interview.
[26]Ibid.
[27]Ibid.

Some of the romantic notions surrounding these artists appear to be accurate, nonetheless. There is most often a truthfulness about them and their work that results from their not being engaged in the politics and ambitions of the world of contemporary art. Other factors in their honesty and lack of pretense relate to their age. Many of the self-taught artists are elderly; when one is seventy or eighty years old, one knows that life is short, and this realization tends to bring an emphasis on spirituality and relationships rather than career advancement. They are also detached from the world of art and its concerns because of their generally rural, small town existence and values rooted in their communities. For example, Murray, being in his seventies and living all of his life in the rural South far from the cultural centers of the world of art, was not motivated by the career values of making a name for himself as an artist, or making money from his art. His values were from his faith and community. He had no concept of art when he began making his marks as he believed God led. In some ways he was introduced to a foreign culture with different values when people from the world of art came to visit him at his home.

Judith McWillie offers another reason why self-taught artists are often more honest in their creative expression. She contends that many artists of the "mainstream" find it difficult to preserve the sincerity of their work because of intrusive demands of making a living through galleries, museums, academia, publishing, and so on. Yet because self-promotion is an economic necessity, mainstream artists generally court these institutions even though they are critical of them. McWillie adds,

> These circumstances [the need to court the art institutions in addition to producing art] create or threaten to create a "divided self," or, at least, a constant source of distraction. The self-taught visionaries were not caught up in this particular schizoid existence, as far as their art was concerned. Thus, to the academically acculturated artist, self-taught art seemed

to be the product of a "wholeness" that they themselves might never achieve.[28]

Murray and most other similar visionaries were not affected and shaped by the history of art and the influence of other artists, but by the social, economic, political, and spiritual circumstances of American life. When one examines the standard Western art historical model used for judging the importance of a contemporary artist's work, it is obvious that Murray, for example, has little relation, as far as his own purpose, to the philosophy that informs and motivates many of the formally trained artists of the so-called "mainstream" world of art. Writer Thomas McEvilley delineates the philosophy that influences many contemporary trained artists and has historically informed the field of Western art history.[29] This Western historic framework and criterion for measuring the importance of an artist's work values art that is

> born out of a strong awareness of the art historical trends that led up to it, that in a sense made it inevitable; it arises out of a fierce determination to add one's own impetus to those developmental trends, and an equally strong awareness of the theoretical issues of the moment and how other artists, one's peers, are dealing with them.[30]

Murray and other similar artists have a different reason for producing their work; the above objective is foreign to the utilitarian impulse and sense of mission that perpetuated their creative drive. Therefore, one best comprehends Murray's art not through the tools of Western art history, but through examining a myriad of cultural forces that influenced him.

---

[28]Judith McWillie, written responses to questions from author, 12 March 1997.
[29]McEvilley, "The Missing Tradition," 137.
[30]Ibid.

The scholarly work of Western art historians and art critics has, until recently, dealt with works of art that fall easily into the continuum of masters and masterpieces identified as making a contribution within a developmental definition of art. For many years, there was an aura of sacredness about the authority of the canon of art history. For the art historian or art critic who believes in the continuum of masters and masterpieces produced by geniuses living within various times in history, it is heresy to believe that a non-literate farm worker such as Murray or a self-proclaimed preacher living in the backwoods of Georgia, like Howard Finster, would be able to produce art with a depth of meaning and formal sophistication equaled to the heroes of Western art.

Many people who had increasingly become disenchanted with contemporary art's self-referential tendencies embraced the self-taught artist because the work emanated from a life involving work, family, and religion to which many people could relate.[31] Similarly, Nasisse says that this art was popular because it often originated from untrained, uneducated people with humble origins. It did not come from the ivory tower: Instead, "[i]t was coming from the farm. It was coming from the ghetto, from the lower class neighborhoods. It was real. It was part of the people. It wasn't isolated and elite. People liked that. Not so much the artists, the academics, but the public loved it."[32] Nasisse also believed that the work was truly inspired and people want that in an artist: "They respect that

---

[31]These artists and their deep spirituality, rural way of life, and their often strong community ties embody some of the foundational values of America that originated in the colonial era and stemmed from Greco-Roman culture and Judeo-Christian morality (Sandler, *Art of the Postmodern Era*, 3.). These values include, as Dave Shi states:

a hostility toward luxury and a suspicion of riches, a reverence for nature and a preference for rural over urban ways of life and work, a desire for personal self-reliance through frugality and diligence, a nostalgia for the past and a skepticism toward the claims of modernity, conscientious rather than conspicuous consumption, and an aesthetic taste for the plain and functional. See Dave E. Shi, *The Simple Life, Plain Living and High Thinking in American Culture* (New York and Oxford: Oxford University Press, 1985), 31.

[32]Nasisse interview, 22 April 1997.

sense of connectedness to something much bigger, that really exists in all of them."[33]

Related to this idea, Judith McWillie, speaking as an artist, writer, and professor of art, states that the final acceptance of the self-taught artists was born out of unfulfilled spiritual aspirations of the initial modernist agenda. McWillie contends that since the 1970s, "mainstream" artists have denied art's moral authority and that much of the art of African-American visionaries, certainly Murray's, reclaims this role and fills an important void.[34]

In addition to offering aesthetically powerful art born of passion, Murray and other self-taught visionary artists commonly exemplified a socially responsive attitude that seeks to reach out to people. In contrast to some more recent modernists' being accused of a valueless pursuit of personal success, Murray and most of these visionaries share what they believe are the most important issues of life.[35] Typically, they hold an idea of success that is based on contributing their talents to the larger community. African-American author Albert Raboteau comments on a philosophy and definition of success that characterizes Murray and many similar artists from the South who are influenced by African beliefs, as well as those inherited in America:

> A greater appreciation of the self as relational might help us perceive the selfish desire for aggrandizement hiding behind many of our images of success. To achieve at the expense of others, from the perspective of traditional African religions, is witchcraft, pure and simple. And if you choose to move too

---

[33]Ibid.

[34]McWillie, written responses.

[35]Modernism did not start out pursuing personal success. Artists such as Matisse, Kandinsky, Cezanne, and Gauguin, to name a few, had idealistic aspirations connected to their art which eschewed materialistic values such as self-promotion. It is the more recent trend (since the 1970s, according to McWillie) of materialism and celebrity that the self-taught artists contrast against in values.

far outside or too far above your community, you risk becoming bewitched.[36]

There exists within many of the self-taught visionaries a pursuit
of wisdom and internal depth, a spiritual power that remains different
from the pursuit of power and recognition in a worldly sense, or power
over others as one forges to the "top" in a career. The power and
effectiveness of visionaries, such as Murray's, emanate from the source
of their vision and often their life of poverty and struggle.

Future Impulses

One must question what specific future impulses the acceptance
of these artists indicates. The self-taught artists have already informed
the contemporary world of art, and many trained artists have been
influenced. They have modified the direction of twentieth century art
away from a rigid formula towards the idea of the individual defining
art rather than the cultural status quo.[37] There now exists an impulse
to look at the work of individuals who in the past did not possess the
proper profile, that is to say, they lack prestigious formal training or
showings in prominent galleries or exhibitions.

The idea of certain kinds of art being more important than others
is also shifting as the boundaries of fine arts and crafts are becoming
less distinct. This separation in the past has often relegated self-taught
artists into a marginal, insignificant role within American art. A
romantic view of particular artists as leaders because of their perceived superiority supports the idea within modernism of the
avant-garde being set apart from the understanding of the general
population. This concept promotes an elitism, based on artistic
sophistication, that contributed to creating the distinctive categories
of high and low arts. The "low" arts were utilitarian, craft oriented,

---

[36]Albert J. Raboteau, "The Black Experience in American Evangelicalism: The Meaning
of Slavery," in *The Evangelical Tradition in America*, Leonard I. Sweet, ed. (Macon GA:
Mercer University Press, 1984), 191.

[37]Nasisse interview, 22 April 1997.

and connected to everyday life. The "high" arts delved into issues of esoteric philosophy and acted as a beacon to move art to new levels of refinement.[38] With the general population having such a lofty view of the artist whose work is connected to esoteric philosophy, it is difficult for artists without training in art or philosophy, and who display a utilitarian, democratic spirit within their work, to be considered significant within the hierarchy of "important" art and artists.

It is not surprising, as the world of art reevaluates romantic beliefs that have supported the narrow idea of heroes who inform the rest of the world of art, that enthusiasm for the work of the self-taught has increased. Yet one must question whether the self-taught visionaries are esteemed as an alternative source of feeding the need for having heroes in art when one sees them as a palliative for certain ills. Does one create an "Other" whose art one can collect, whose life can be romanticized, yet who is ultimately seen as a lesser artist? Time can only tell whether their place in American art, after this wave of enthusiasm, is as minor artists who have little of importance to contribute. One must question whether their homespun directness and religious expression that intrigues initially will later be a cause for marginalization.

---

[38]One of the sources of the idea of the avant-garde artist being a savior and one who pulls the less enlightened up with his wisdom is the German philosopher Frederick Nietzsche's (1844-1900) concept of the "Ubermensch." To Nietzsche, the Ubermensch of each era brought society forward through teaching and example. Various modern artists were affected by this concept and related the idea to the world of art. Wassily Kandinsky's book, *Concerning the Spiritual in Art*, supports the idea of the artist savior:

> But there never fails to come to the rescue some human being, like ourselves in everything except that he has in him a secret power of vision. He sees and points the way. The power to do this he would sometimes fain lay aside, for it is a bitter cross to bear. But he cannot do so. Scorned and hated, he drags after him over the stones the heavy chariot of a divided humanity, ever forwards and upwards. See Wassily Kandinsky, *Concerning the Spiritual in Art and Painting in Particular*, Michael Sadleir, Francis Goffling, Michael Harrison, and Ferdinand Ostertag, trans. The Documents of Moderns Art series (1912; New York: Wittenborn, 1947).

The reception of the broadening of the canon of art spurred on by the philosophy of "multiculturalism" has had varying receptions from those who fear the loss of a past philosophy that produced an impressive line of work through its masters and masterpieces. Some see the changes in the future as involving the gradual adding of diverse groups of artists and including them in the present art establishment. Others believe that the philosophy behind the past elitism needs to be overthrown and a new way of viewing artists commence. Still others allow for the past canon and its philosophy to continue while other traditions of equal importance exist in parallel and occasionally interfacing directions.

In the past, as the world of art developed its own system of values and judgments, it cultivated a self-referential system unchecked by outside counsel. Increasingly the world of art developed its own language and its own scheme of exclusions. According to writer Kenneth Ames, its constituency seemed "to have drifted particularly far off into their own rarefied, jargonistic dream worlds, ever more distant from the world of real speaking, acting, touching, living people and their concerns."[39] In contrast, the work of the self-taught enhances our understanding of the many functions art can serve. One hopes that life, popular culture, and fine art will become less distinct categories so that art can broaden the democratic impulse.

The Art of J. B. Murray

J. B. Murray was moved by his conviction of a revelation, not simply a religion. Consequently, in addition to Murray's art, this study concerns a spirit—a compelling energy that affected him and, through him, touched others. Murray sought to communicate a seemingly indecipherable impulse born of a Christian world view that had the prime mission of offering spiritual healing and salvation through

---

[39]Kenneth Ames, "Outside the Outsider Art," *The Artist Outsider: Creativity and the Boundaries of Culture*, Michael D. Hall and Eugene W. Metcalf, Jr. with Roger Cardinal, eds. (Washington and London: Smithsonian Institution Press, 1994), 259.

attention to the warnings embedded in his images. In Murray's work, one witnesses the results of an unseen stimulus that compelled him to create nebulous figures trapped in a chaotic storm and mysterious writing that, according to him, comprised "the language of the Holy Spirit direct from God."[40] Murray's tightly packed compositions indicate a predicament of entrapment and brilliant colors with points of pigment, like beads, convey his concept of a material obsession that Murray believed too often eclipsed the care of the soul. Murray expressed a world full of empty individuals, a world out of control due to its alienation from the Holy. Nevertheless, his underlying structure insinuates his belief in a divine rule that undergirds all of life. Disorder exists, but not hopelessness. As Murray presented us with his figures caught and flung around helplessly in dynamic compositions, he told of the hope of salvation. He believed God led him to depict lost souls as a warning, offering the chance of repentance for those whose eyes could open.

Murray's art offers the product of an intense emotional and perhaps mystical state. This very primacy and singleness of purpose characteristic of an evangelical understanding gave Murray and his work the endowment of a direct, focused perception and objective. His use of dots, dashes, and energetic markings in his art, such as seen in color plate 7, and the fervent sprawl of script on the outside of his house, seen in illustration 3, demonstrate his frenetic zeal and energy that gave his work visual power.

Artists have been moved to express their Christian faith for two thousand years. Murray does not confer a new religious dogma expressed through art; what he does impart is an example of an artist so consumed with a vision he wanted to bestow that he extended his entire existence to communicate through abstract forms emanating out of a profoundly religious subconscious. He sets forth an example of drive and passion for a cause beyond himself, deeper than his human ego. His delicate though intense paintings act as conveyors of

---

[40]Transcript (in author's possession) of J. B. Murray, interview with Judith McWillie, video recording, Mitchell GA, 31 May 1986.

a spiritual consciousness as he asserted an eternal awareness and the enigma of human destiny through the form of limbless, helpless figures. His evangelical faith is not esoteric. Murray did not hold himself apart from his audience but acted as their emissary for expressing a mystical essence to whoever could receive the message of his art: "This well is deep and never go dry."

BIBLIOGRAPHY

Books and Articles

Another Face of the Diamond: Pathways Through the Black Atlantic South. Catalogue for the exhibition *Another Face of the Diamond: Pathways Through the Black Atlantic South.* 23 January-3 March, 1989. Atlanta GA: New Visions Gallery of Contemporary Art; New York: Intar Latin American Gallery, 1989.

Austin, Allan D. *African Muslims in Ante-bellum America—A Source book.* New York and London: Garland Publishing, Inc., 1984.

Bravmann, René A. *African Islam.* Washington DC: The Smithsonian Institute Press; London and Great Britain: Ethnographica Ltd., 1983.

Cardinal, Roger. "Figures and Faces in Outsider Art." In *Portraits From the Outside: Outsider Art—Art Brut,* 28. New York: Grœgfeax Publishing, 1990. Catalogue for the exhibition *Portraits From the Outside: Figurative Expression in Outsider Art,* 7-30 November 1990, Parsons School of Design Gallery.

Carr, Simon. "A Connecting Thread." In *Portraits From the Outside: Outsider Art—Art Brut.* New York: Grœgfeax Publishing, 1990. Catalogue for the exhibition *Portraits From the Outside: Figurative Expression in Outsider Art,* 7-30 November 1990, Parsons School of Design Gallery.

————. "The Visionary Body." In *Portraits From the Outside: Outsider Art—Art Brut,* 48. New York: Grœgfeax Publishing, 1990. Catalogue for the exhibition *Portraits From the Outside: Figurative Expression in Outsider Art,* 7-30 November 1990, Parsons School of Design Gallery.

Courtine, Jean-Jacques. "Raw Bodies." In *Portraits From the Outside: Outsider Art—Art Brut,* 37. Translated by J. Landy. New York: Grœgfeax Publishing, 1990. Catalogue for the exhibition *Portraits From the Outside: Figurative Expression in Outsider Art,* 7-30 November 1990, Parsons School of Design Gallery.

Emerson, Ralph Waldo. "The Poet." In *The Collected Works of Ralph Waldo Emerson*. Volume 3. Cambridge: Belnap Press, 1983.

Farber, Sam. "Portraits from the Outside." In *Portraits From the Outside: Outsider Art—Art Brut*, 7. New York: Grœgfeax Publishing, 1990. Catalogue for the exhibition *Portraits From the Outside: Figurative Expression in Outsider Art*, 7-30 November 1990, Parsons School of Design Gallery.

Foy, James L. and James P. McMurrer. "James Hampton, Artist and Visionary." In *Transcultural Aspects of Psychiatric Art*, 720. Edited by Irene Jakab. Volume 4 of Psychiatry and Art series. New York: Karger and Bisel, 1975.

Moore, Thomas. "The Liminal Zones of the Soul." In Suzi Gablik, *Conversations Before the End of Time*, 409. New York NY: Thames and Hudson Inc., 1995.

Hall, Michael D. and Eugene W. Metcalf, Jr., with Roger Cardinal. *The Artist Outsider: Creativity and the Boundaries of Culture*. Smithsonian Institution Press: Washington and London, 1994.

Hill, Samuel S., editor. *Encyclopedia of Religion in the South*. Macon GA: Mercer University Press, 1984.

Jacobs, Joseph. *A World of Their Own: Twentieth-Century American Folk Art*. Newark: The Newark Museum, 1995.

Johnson, Ken. "Significant Others," *Art in America* (June 1993): 87.

Judy, Ronald A. T. *(Dis) Forming the American Canon—African-Arabic Slave Narratives and the Vernacular*. Minneapolis: The University of Minnesota Press, 1993.

Kandinsky, Wassily. *Concerning the Spiritual in Art and Painting in Particular*. Translated by Michael Sadleir, Francis Goffling, Michael Harrison, and Ferdinand Ostertag. The Documents of Moderns Art series. 1912. Reprint, New York: Wittenborn, 1947.

Kurtz, Bruce D. *Contemporary Art 1965-1990*. Englewood Cliffs NJ: Prentice Hall, 1992.

Lincoln, C. Eric. "The American Muslim Mission in the Context of American Social History," in *The Muslim Community in North America*. Edited by Earle H. Waugh, Baha Abu-Laban and Regula B. Queshi. Edmonton: The University of Alberta Press, 1983.

MacGregor, John M. "Marginal Outsider." In *Portraits From the Outside: Outsider Art—Art Brut*. New York: Grœgfeax Publishing, 1990. Catalogue for the exhibition *Portraits From the Outside: Figurative Expression in Outsider Art*, 7-30 November 1990, Parsons School of Design Gallery.

Marsden, George M. "Fundamentalism and American Evangelicalsim." In *The Variety of American Evangelicalism*, 22. Dayton, Donald W. and Robert K. Johnson, editors. Knoxville: The University of Tennessee Press, 1991.

Mathews, Donald G. *Religion in the Old South*. Chicago and London: The University of Chicago Press, 1977.

McEvilley, Thomas. "The Missing Tradition." *Art in America* (May 1997): 79, 137.

McWillie, Judith. "Another Face of the Diamond: Black Traditional Art from the Deep South." *The Clarion* (Fall 1987): 42.

————. *Even the Deep Things of God: A Quality of Mind in Afro-Atlantic Traditional Art*. Pittsburg: Pittsburgh Center for the Arts, 1990.

Mhire, Herman, Andy Nasisse, and Maude Wahlman. *Baking in the Sun—Visionary Images from the South: Selections from the Collection of Sylvia and Warren Lowe*. Lafayette: University Art Museum; University of Southwestern Louisiana, 1987.

Murray, J. B. "This Well Is Deep and Never Go Dry—The Work of J. B. Murray." Interview with Andy Nasisse. In *Portraits From the Outside: Outsider Art—Art Brut*. New York: Grœgfeax Publishing, 1990. Catalogue for the exhibition *Portraits From the Outside: Figurative Expression in Outsider Art*, 7-30 November 1990, Parsons School of Design Gallery.

Parrindes, E. G. *African Traditional Religion*. London: Sheldon Press, 1974.

Perry, Regina. "John B. Murry." In *Pictured in My Mind: Contemporary American Self-Taught Art*, 150. Birmingham: Birmingham Museum of Art, 1995.

Raboteau, Albert J. *A Fire in the Bones*. Boston: Beacon Press, 1995.

Sandler, Irving. *Art of the Post-Modern Era: From the Late 1960s to the Early 1990s*. New York: Harper Collins Publisher, Inc., 1996.

Sernett, Milton C. *Afro-American Religious History: A Documentary Witness*. Durham NC: Duke University Press, 1985.

Sweet, Leonard I. *The Evangelical Tradition in America*. Macon GA: Mercer University Press, 1984.

Thevoz, Michel and Allen S. Weiss. "Art Brut." In *Portraits From the Outside: Outsider Art—Art Brut*. New York: Grœgfeax Publishing, 1990. Catalogue for the exhibition *Portraits From the Outside: Figurative Expression in Outsider Art*, 7-30 November 1990, Parsons School of Design Gallery.

Thompson, Robert Farris. *"Writings Witnessed through the Waters:" Remarks on the work of J. B. Murray*. Invitation for the exhibition *Outsider Gallery, the Rosa Esman Gallery*. New York. 29 April-17 May, 1985. New York: Rosa Esman Gallery, 1985.

Weber, Timothy P. "Premillennialism and the Branches of Evangelicalism." In *The Variety of American Evangelicalism*, 12. Dayton, Donald W. and Robert K. Johnson, editors. Knoxville: The University of Tennessee Press, 1991.

Weiss, Allen S. "Figurations and Disfigurations." In *Portraits From the Outside: Outsider Art—Art Brut*. New York: Grœgfeax Publishing, 1990. Catalogue for the exhibition *Portraits From the Outside: Figurative Expression in Outsider Art*, 7-30 November 1990, Parsons School of Design Gallery.

Yelen, Alice Rae. *Passionate Visions of the American South*. New Orleans: New Orleans Museum of Art, 1993.

Interviews

Arnett, William. Conversation with author. Atlanta GA, 10 June 1995.

Berman, Rick. Interview with author. Transcript. Berman Gallery. Atlanta GA, 20 May 1994.

———. Written response to questions from author. 10 March 1997.

Cubbs, Joanne. Phone interview with author. Tape recording. 25 April 1997.

Eiland, William. Interview with author. Tape recording. Athens GA, 12 June 1997.

Fordham, Carolyn. Interview with author. Tape recording. Mitchell GA, 20 July 1993.

Godlass, Allen. Interview with author. Transcript. Athens GA, 16 March 1993.

Ingram, Ernest. Telephone conversation with author, 20 July 1993.

Lamar, Krista. Telephone conversation with author, 25 February 1995.

———. Telephone conversation with author, 22 December 1995.

Lundy, Leona. Interview with author. Tape recording. Mitchell GA, 20 July 1993.

McWillie, Judith. Telephone conversation with author, 28 June 1993.

———. Telephone conversation with author, 4 August 1993.

———. Interview with author. Transcript. Athens GA, 4 April 1994.

———. Interview with author. Transcript. Athens GA, 10 January 1995.

———. Written responses to questions from author. 12 March 1997.

———. Telephone conversation with author. 31 January 2000.

Murray, J. B. Interview with Judith McWillie. Mitchell GA, 31 May 1986. Transcribed by author from video recording.

Nasisse, Andy. Interview with author. Tape recording. Athens GA, 30 June 1993.

———. Telephone conversation with author, 5 June 1994.

———. Interview with author. Tape recording. Athens GA, 18 January 1995.

————. Interview with author. Tape recording. Athens GA, 22 April 1997.

Pinkston, Sara Murray. Interview with author. Tape recording. Mitchell GA, 20 July 1993.

Rawlings, William. Interview with author. Tape recording. Sandersville GA, 1 May 1993.

————. Interview with author. Tape recording. Sandersville GA, 3 June 1993.

————. Telephone conversation with author, 17 January 1996.

Spalding, Phinizy. Telephone conversation with author, 1 July 1993.

Tucker, Larry. Interview with author. Tape recording. Mitchell GA, 20 July 1993.

Tucker, Nathaniel. Interview with author. Tape recording. Mitchell GA, 20 July 1993.